Beginner's Guide to Quilting

For Jude and Florence

Beginner's Guide to Quilting

16 Projects to Learn to Quilt

Elizabeth Betts

David and Charles

www.stitchcraftcreate.co.uk

Contents

Introduction	7
Tools and Equipment	8
Fabric	10

Techniques

Piecing	16
Rotary cutting	21
Making a quilt sandwich	23
Quilting	24
Binding	28

Projects

	30
Patchwork Rosette Needle Book	32
Flowered Dolly's Quilt	36
Tote-ally Fabulous Bag	40
Simple Seedheads Table Mat	44
Checkerboard Charms Car Quilt	48
Summer Delight Table Runner	54
Spinning Around Cushion	60
Twirling Windmills Quilt	66
Scooter Strips Wall Hanging	72
Here and There Quilt	78
Box du Jour	84
Grab and Sew Quilt	88
Summer Sunburst Cushion	94
Funky Town Wall Hanging	100
Spots and Blocks Bookmarks	106
Blooming Marvellous Bed Quilt	110

Templates	118
Glossary	122
Acknowledgements	124
About the Author	125
Suppliers	126
Index	127

Introduction

Welcome to my world of patchwork and quilting – your journey starts here!

In my quilt business I meet people every day who fancy making a quilt, but don't know where to start. Then there are others who have started making a quilt, then got stuck and popped in for some advice as a last resort before putting their half-made quilt in the loft. If you recognize yourself as fitting into one of these categories then this book is for you. The projects have been designed to be easy and accessible, with the difficulty increasing gradually as the book goes on. If you work through them all in order, you will develop a wide range of techniques.

The projects are also suitable for those who want to make a quick quilt, or experiment with a technique they haven't tried before, such as using a jelly roll or machine quilting. The smaller projects can make excellent presents.

Don't be daunted by the idea of learning a new skill. I have tried to make the tone of the book friendly rather than authoritative, as if a friend was talking you through the projects. I believe the process of making is as important as the finished result. Through trial and error, you will find a way that suits you – if it works for you then it is fine. Enjoy the process!

Quilts have been made for hundreds of years, so the process of making a quilt connects you with the past, while making something for the future at the same time. Investing time in quilting is a relaxing antidote to today's throwaway culture. I like to think of each quilt I give away as giving the recepient a hug every time they snuggle up under it.

My journey in quilt making started with a chance encounter eleven years ago. I made my first item, a patchwork bag, and something clicked. I found that playing with pattern and fabric became utterly addictive, which is how I now find myself here. I hope you get hooked too.

Happy quilting!

Tools and Equipment

It can be appealing to buy lots of haberdashery when you start making patchwork. I suggest you begin with a hand sewing kit, then buy other sewing tools as and when you need them. A good basic hand sewing kit should contain needles, thread, scissors, thimble, pins, tape measure and seam ripper. Keep your sewing kit in a box. There are some pretty ones available to buy, although a toolbox from a DIY store does the job just as well! It is also worth having a notebook and pencil handy when sewing to jot down notes and ideas as you stitch.

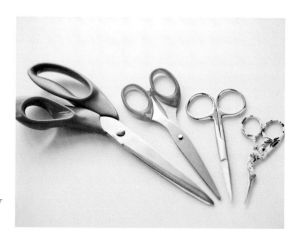

Basic kit

Needles: Use Sharps for hand piecing, and embroidery or chenille needles for hand quilting with perle thread. Buy a pack of needles with different sizes so you can try them to see which one you feel most comfortable using.

Thread: Make sure you buy a good brand from a sewing shop as it will be colour-fast and you will be less likely to have tension issues with your sewing machine. For piecing cotton fabric it is best to use 50-weight 100 per cent cotton thread. Natural colours, such as light grey or beige, tend to tone with most fabrics, so buy them on large reels to save money and trips to the shop to buy more thread when you run out. For big stitch hand quilting, I use perle thread in a size 8. For machine quilting, look for threads specially made for this purpose as they will be stronger.

Scissors: It is handy to have at least two pairs: a large pair for cutting fabric, and a small pair for snipping threads. It is also good to keep a pair of paper scissors in your sewing box so you aren't tempted to use your fabric scissors on template plastic or paper as this will blunt them.

Thimble: These are available in metal, plastic and even leather. Try out different styles and sizes to see what suits you.

Pins: Different types of pins are available, but for patchwork look for long, fine pins. Flower- or glass-headed pins are handy if you work in a space also used by children or pets, as you can spot them easily if you drop them.

Tape measure: A standard tape measure is fine; however, if you plan to make large quilts, look for an extra long (120in/300cm) one.

Seam ripper: This is an essential tool for unpicking seams quickly.

Notebook and pencil: These are handy to keep nearby when sewing to make notes on, for example, colour of thread used, size of stitch, or ideas that come to mind while sewing.

Other quilting tools

Marking tools: These are used to mark sewing or quilting lines on the fabric. The types most widely used are:
Chalk based – pencils, tailor's chalk, propelling pencils.
Pens – water-soluble or vanishing pens.
Adhesive tape – low-tack masking tape, ¼in (0.6cm) wide.
Pressure based – the Hera marker uses a pressure to mark quilting lines.

Template plastic: This is a sheet of a strong plastic that is used to make patchwork or quilting templates.

Quilter's safety pins: These are normally curved to make using them easier. They hold the layers of the quilt together ready for quilting.

Rotary cutter: If you are machine piecing, one of these is essential. Rotary cutters come in several sizes, but the 45mm is the one most widely used for patchwork (see p21 for more information).

Self-healing mat: An A2 size mat is the most useful, as it comfortably fits a piece of 44in (110cm) wide fabric folded in half. I also find an A3 size handy if sewing at home on a small table (see page 21 for more information).

Acrylic ruler: Rulers come in many different shapes and sizes, from small 4in (10.2cm) squares to hexagons and circles (see page 21 for more information).

Sewing machine: There are some lovely sewing machines marketed at quilters; however, all you need to start is a basic sewing machine that sews a straight stitch. If you are trying patchwork for the first time, it may be that you can borrow a sewing machine, which will give you a better idea of what you are looking for when it comes to buying one. For quilt making using a sewing machine, it is handy to buy a ¼in (0.6cm) foot, a darning foot and a walking foot to go with the standard feet that come with your machine. More details of these are given in the machine piecing and machine quilting sections (see pages 19 and 27). You can get useful advice from specialist sewing machine shops, which will usually let you try one out. Some features, such as needle up/down, speed control and the ability to machine sew a blanket stitch, are handy to have, but these are not essential.

Fabric

Choosing fabric can be one of the most exciting parts of making a quilt. People sometimes describe the feeling of going into a quilt shop as being similar to their childhood experience of walking into a sweet shop – so many lovely things they want to buy! Other people can find it stressful, and get worried about buying fabric that is wrong or doesn't go together. Remember, fabric choice is a personal thing, so don't get swayed by over-enthusiastic shop assistants or friends. If you like it, then use it.

The essentials

When you are starting out in quilt making, try to use 100 per cent craft-weight cotton. Yes, that vintage silk quilt you saw at a museum is lovely, but it is easier to get to grips with the basics using craft-weight cotton before moving on to more challenging fabric. Likewise, avoid using polycotton at first; however, with a bit of perseverance and practice, any fabric can be made into a quilt. Recycling old clothes and sheets, particularly when they remind you of a loved one, is great, but try to match the fabrics so they are of a similar weight. If you are unsure of what to buy, take your time to choose. Visit your local quilt shop to touch the fabric. Try to buy the best quality you can afford. If you are on a budget, look out for sales or remnant sections. Another tip to save money is to mix expensive prints with plain fabrics that tend to be cheaper.

Craft-weight cotton is usually sold from bolts that are 44in (110cm) wide. You can buy any quantity of fabric from the bolt, from 10in (25cm) upwards. Lots of quilters like to use a cut of fabric called a 'fat quarter'. Fat quarters are sold in both metric and imperial measurements. Metric fat quarters are made from 0.5m of fabric cut in half across the middle, so they measure 50cm x 55cm. You can also buy long quarters that are 25 x 110cm. Imperial fat quarters are slightly smaller. They are made from 1/2yd of fabric cut in half across the middle, so they measure 18in x 22in (45.7cm x 55.9cm). Some fabrics are available in extra wide lengths (usually 90in/230cm or 108in/274cm); these are excellent to use as quilt backings as you don't then have to piece fabric together.

Some quilters pre-wash their fabrics before using them, and others don't. Fabric from good quality manufacturers should be colour-fast, but it is worth giving all fabrics a quick wash and dry before using them just to make sure.

Colour

Colour is a personal thing. Everyone has colours they love and hate, but try to keep an open mind. Despite dressing well and having tasteful homes, it is amazing the number of quilters who say they can't 'do' colour. To get inspiration for using colour, look around you. Magazines, particularly interior and garden ones, can be good for showing some unusual colour combinations. Pink and green are a great combination you often see in nature, and blues and greens can be seen anywhere there is water.

One way I put colour combinations together is to choose a fabric I love, one with a strong print and lots of colours in it, and then match other fabrics from that starting point. If you are matching fabrics to a project over time, it can be useful to cut off a small piece and attach it to a card to keep in your purse. That way you are not carrying a bundle of fabric everywhere you go (this is particularly useful when at a quilt show). Other people find it helpful to cut the part of the selvedge off where there are the small dots with numbers on them. These are the colour references for the screen so you see all the colours used.

If you are buying from a quilt shop, take fabrics to the window to see them in natural daylight. When buying fabrics from the internet, take into consideration that your computer screen may not give you a true representation of the colour. If you are matching colours to a specific project, contact the supplier, as most are happy for you to send them a swatch to compare, or buy a smaller piece before splashing out on metres of it.

Bundles and pre-cuts are a useful way to buy fabric and one where you don't have to worry about colour. Bundles are packs of fabric, either fat quarters or half metres, which go well together. Sometimes they are all from one designer's range or the shop can have put the colour combination together. Pre-cuts are packs of fabrics that have been cut to a specific size. The most common one is the Charm Pack, which contains 5in (12.7cm) squares. Also well known are Jelly Rolls, which are strips measuring 2½in x 44in (6.3cm x 110cm), and Layer Cakes that are 10in (25.4cm) squares. Buying these packs can speed up the process of choosing fabric, give you confidence that the fabrics will co-ordinate, and they can save you money if you want to work with lots of different colours and prints.

The tone of the fabric can be as important as its colour. Many quilts look best if you use a combination of light, medium and dark fabrics. If in doubt as to which fabric is light and which is dark, try photographing them together and turning the picture into a black and white image. Sometimes you can be surprised that the fabric you thought of as the dark one is actually one of the lighter ones.

Prints can also help to personalize a quilt if you are making it for someone else. This can be as obvious as trains for a child who likes them, or apple fabric for a couple who got married in New York. Also, consider the overall feel of a quilt when the prints are put together. For a quilt with a fifties vintage feel, a variety of prints can be used, such as florals, spots and stripes, whereas adding a striking digital print of a computer would not go with the overall feel.

If you are interested in print, many of the quilt fabric designers have blogs that explain their inspiration and work process for their ranges. If you buy some fabric you like, check whether the designer's name is on the selvedge and then do an internet search to see if they have a website.

The scale of print can be important in patchwork. For example, a large-scale print may get lost when cut into smaller pieces, but can look fabulous when used as a focal point for the quilt, or for a quilt backing where its full potential can be seen. There is a theory that the smaller the patchwork the smaller the print should be, but this does not always apply: remember, rules are made to be broken!

Pattern

Once you have started buying fabric, you will quickly discover the type of patterns you prefer. For example, I love a cheeky novelty print and can never leave a quilt shop or show without one! Other people love a specific print, such as leaves. Go with your passion and you will soon start collecting your very own stash. It is a good idea to collect a range of stash builders/blenders. These can be spots, checks or tone-on-tone fabrics, but they can be invaluable to have on hand to mix in with more vibrant prints. They are not usually the fabrics that will attract your eye at first, but they always end up being used.

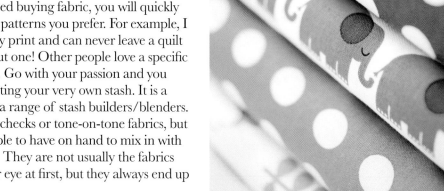

Wadding (batting)

Wadding (batting) is the middle layer of a quilt. It provides warmth and, once quilted, adds texture. It can be bought off the roll, or pre-packed in different sizes. If buying the latter, lay it out on a bed for a day before using it to get rid of any creases.

Most waddings (battings) shrink when you first wash them, and the label will tell by what percentage. If you like the wrinkled vintage look that's great; however, if you don't, it is best to pre-wash your wadding (batting). The label will also tell you how far apart it needs to be quilted. It is important not to ignore this information as the wadding (batting) can start to break up after repeated washes if you do not put enough quilting stitches through the quilt. You can now buy wadding (batting) that can be quilted up to 10in (25.4cm) apart, so if you are not planning on doing a lot of quilting look out for this type. The word 'loft' refers to how thick the wadding (batting) is; you can buy very thin loft wadding (batting) as well as very thick.

The majority of waddings (battings) are cream in colour, but you can get white or black types. If you are making a project in black fabric, it is essential to use dark wadding (batting) as cream wadding (batting) can lighten it; likewise use cream wadding (batting) for quilts made with paler fabric as dark wadding (batting) would dull the finished quilt..

You can buy wadding (batting) that contains different fibre contents. Many shops sell sample packs, which means you can try different types and see which one you prefer. Cotton and polyester are the most popular ones to use. One type that is particularly soft and lovely to work with is 100 per cent cotton, but it is not the easiest wadding (batting) to hand quilt, so make sure you have a sharp needle and thimble to hand. Polyester is durable and easy to hand quilt, but is quite stiff and can get very warm. I use it mainly for wall hangings. Cotton/polyester blends are popular with those who both machine quilt and hand quilt and like the durability of polyester with the softness of cotton. You can also buy wool, silk, soy, bamboo and recycled wadding (batting).

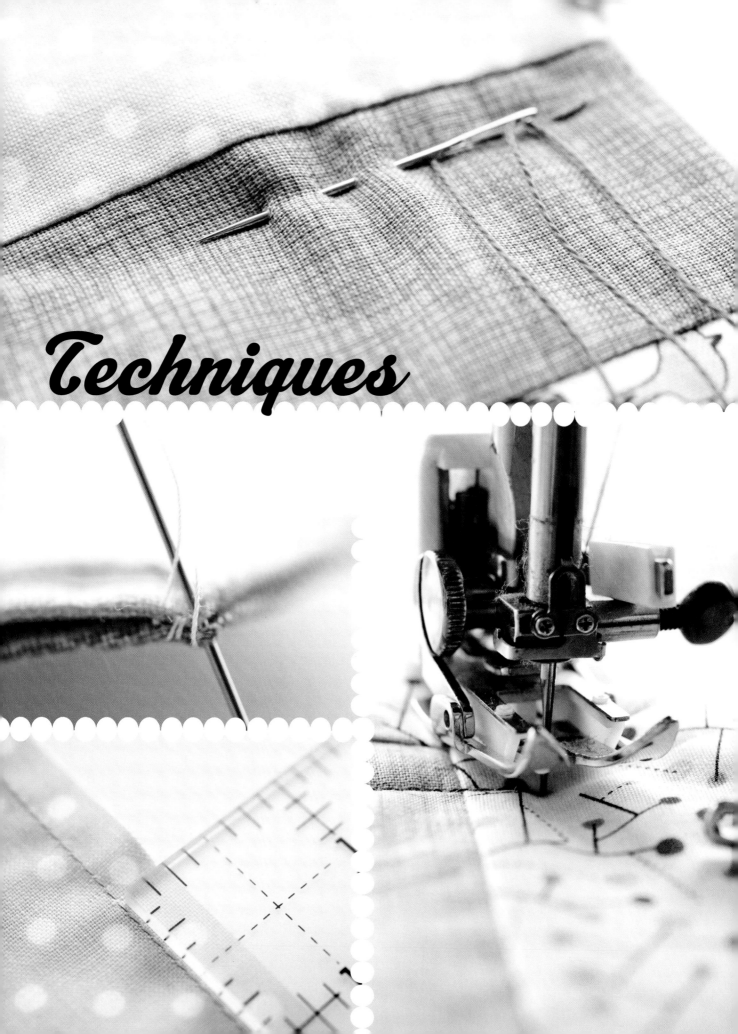

Techniques

Piecing

In patchwork, piecing is the term used for sewing fabric together. It can be done by hand, or on the machine. Try piecing using both methods to see what suits you.

When piecing together fabrics that are different colours, use thread in a beige or grey colour as your eye will not be drawn to it like it would be for a white thread. When I find a neutral colour that works, I buy large reels as it is economical and convenient. If making a quilt with fabrics in predominantly one colour, say blue, I would then use a mid-blue colour thread.

For piecing, use 100 per cent cotton, 50-weight thread as it is suitable for both hand and machine piecing, and easy to find.

Hand piecing

Sewing patchwork by hand is really enjoyable. It is often portable so you can work for an hour in the evening in front of the television, then take it into work and do another 30 minutes on it in your lunch break. It has a reputation for being slow to do, but hand sewing while doing another activity means it uses 'down time'. Is's faster to piece on the sewing machine, but if you don't have a dedicated sewing room where you can keep your machine set up, it is much more convenient to have sewing you can pick up and put down.

Keep everything you need in a small box, such as a pretty vintage tin, then all you have to do is open the tin and start sewing where you left off. I use Sharps needles for hand piecing. Buy a pack of needles that contains different sizes and try different ones to see which one suits you.

The most important thing about hand piecing is to make sure that the beginning and end of your seam are really secure. If you are making something to be quilted after it is hand pieced, this will add to the strength of the item.

The two methods of piecing that I use are English paper piecing and American block patchwork piecing.

English paper piecing

This technique tacks (bastes) fabric to paper shapes, which are then oversewn. It is good for making patchwork with different regular shapes, such as hexagons and diamonds, hence it is also sometimes known as mosaic patchwork.

1 Make a template out of card or template plastic. Draw round the template on to paper – scrap paper is fine – and cut out the shape from the paper.

2 Pin the paper piece to the back of the fabric. Using scissors, cut around the shape, leaving a generous ¼in (0.6cm) seam allowance all around.

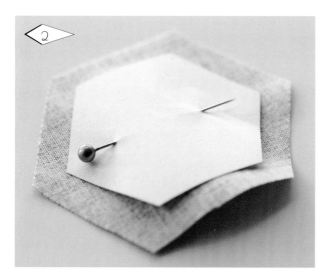

3 Thread a needle and tie a knot in the end. Fold the seam allowance over the piece of paper and tack (baste) in place using a large running stitch.

4 Place two patches on top of each other, right sides together. To oversew the patches together, thread a needle and start ¼in (0.6cm) in from the edge of the piece where you want to start, and take a few tiny stitches back to the edge, which serves as a backstitch to secure the thread. Then work your way along the seam and sew a few reverse stitches at the end of the fabric to secure. Keep sewing the patches together in this manner. If you are making a large quilt, work in small units then join them together later.

5 When you have finished making the patchwork, take out the tacking (basting) stitches and the paper backing. Keep the paper backings as they can be used for another project.

American block patchwork piecing

In this method you draw a line on the back of the fabric, which is then used as a guideline to sew along using a small running stitch.

1 To make your template, draw your shape on to card or template plastic.

2 Place your fabric on a table, right side down. Place the template on top and draw around it using a pencil. The template does not include a seam allowance, so draw another line ¼in (0.6cm) away from the first line. You can buy rulers made to this width for this purpose.

3 Take two pieces, and place them right sides together. Insert a pin at each end of the row, making sure it goes through the drawn line on both pieces of fabric. If it is a long seam, insert as many pins along the row as needed to ensure the pencil lines on the top and bottom fabric line up.

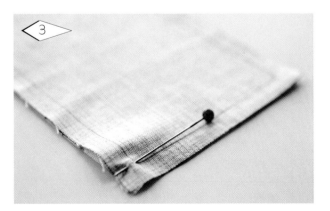

4 Thread a needle with approximately 18in (45.7cm) of thread (no more than this or it will tangle up as you sew). Knot the end, then sew a small running stitch along the line. If you are sewing a long seam, do a backstitch along it approximately every 5in (12.7cm) to make the line of stitching stonger. If you are joining two rows together that already have seams where pieces of fabric have been sewn together, stitch along the row then, when you get to a seam, take a backstitch. Then place the needle through the seam and, instead of sewing it down, take a backstitch, and carry on sewing.

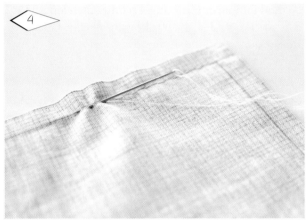

5 When you get to the end, finish with a small backstitch. Press the seam together as this helps to make it stronger.

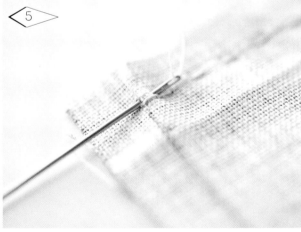

Machine piecing

Speed is the main reason for the popularity of machine piecing. If you don't have anywhere to keep a sewing machine out, it can feel a hassle setting up (as opposed to hand piecing where you just open a box). On the plus side, you can whizz though lots of sewing in an afternoon when using a machine. If you cut fabric carefully with a rotary cutter, and sew the pieces together with an accurate seam allowance, you will get a piece of patchwork that fits together perfectly.

Any sewing machine that can sew a straight stitch can be used for machine piecing. I set the stitch length to 2.2, and use a 70/12 or 80/12 jeans needle. Change the needle for each new project.

With machine piecing, the first thing you need to do is work out where your ¼in (0.6cm) seam allowance is. If you get this seam allowance accurate, it helps your sewing match up. Most sewing machines have a foot you can buy that has a ¼in (0.6cm) guide on it, so you just need to line the fabric up with the edge of the foot when sewing.

Alternatively, if you do not have one of these, you can line up a piece of scrap fabric with the edge of the foot, sew a short line of stitches, then take the fabric out and measure the distance between the edge of the fabric and the sewn line. If it is not ¼in (0.6cm), move the position of your needle by

changing the width setting on your sewing machine. Unless the pattern says, there is no need to do a reverse stitch at the beginning or end of a seam. Test again, and then keep doing this until you have it right. Another idea is to use a strip of low-tack masking tape on the sewing machine. Write the correct settings in a notebook so you can get your machine set up quickly each time you want to sew.

Chain piecing

Chain piecing is where pieces of fabric are sewn together, without cutting the threads at the end of each separate piece of fabric. It is quick, and can save on thread too.

1 Line up two pieces of fabric, right sides together.

2 Place them under the presser foot, just before the needle.

3 Hold the threads to the back and sew along the seam, making sure you guide the fabric rather than pull it through the machine. There is no need to make a reverse stitch at the beginning or end of chain piecing.

4 When you get to the end of the fabric, stop sewing with the needle down. Lift the presser foot and lay the next piece of fabric to be sewn.

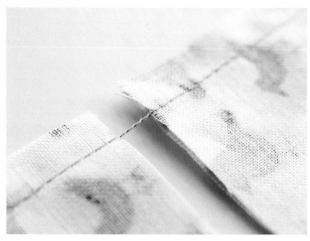

Lower the presser foot and carefully start sewing again. There should be a couple of stitches sewn between the fabric. When you have finished your sewing, take the line of fabric from the machine, and cut the thread in between each piece.

Tips on pressing

With machine piecing, you can either press the seams together, or press them open. There are pros and cons to each method. Pressing seams open can make the quilt lie flatter, but it can be weaker than when pressing them together. I have pressed the seams together in the projects in this book, but use the finish you like best.

The best way to press is to iron from the front to set the seam, then turn the fabric over and press the seam in place. Turn the fabric over and iron the front of the seam again, making sure the patchwork is nice and flat.

Rotary cutting

The first few projects in this book are sewn by hand, and can be made without a rotary cutter, mat and ruler. However, if you get hooked on quilting, then a set is an essential piece of kit.

If looked after, they should last a long time. The only extra item you will need to buy is a replacement blade for your rotary cutter when it starts to blunt.

Rotary cutter: These come in a few sizes, but the 45mm is the one most widely used for patchwork. There are different types, so see if you can try a few before deciding on which one to buy.

Self-healing mat: Make sure you store your mat flat as it can warp. Mats have measurements on them in inches or centimetres, but I usually only use the measurements on my acrylic ruler.

Acrylic ruler: I find the most useful ruler to use is a long, rectangular ruler measuring 24in x 6½in. This is long enough to cut 44in (110cm) wide fabric folded in half. I find a 12½in (31.7cm) square and a 6in (15.2cm) square handy to have too. Rulers are available in both imperial and metric measurements; however, I would use them as you would a recipe – don't mix the two on the same project.

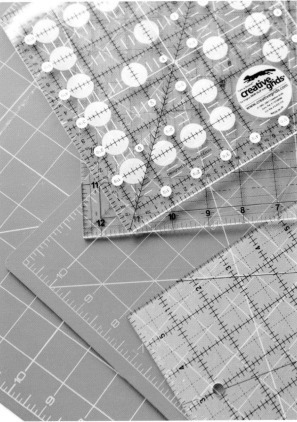

Cutting strips and squares

Adapt this method to whatever size of square, rectangle or strip you need to cut. Once you have got used to using the equipment, you will find it a quick and accurate way of cutting fabric.

The instructions below are for a single layer of fabric; you can, however, cut several layers with a rotary cutter. When cutting layers, keep them lined up by spinning the board round so it is in the right position to cut, rather than lifting up the fabric as it will shift and make your next cut less accurate.

To help cut the fabric on the straight of the grain, line up the bottom of the ruler with the selvedge for the first cut. Then trim off the selvedge and put this to one side, so you don't accidentally use a piece of fabric that has the selvedge on it in the quilt. The selvedge also pulls in the fabric near it, so cutting it off helps the fabric relax and lay flat.

Before you start, read through the safety tips.

1 Lay the fabric on a cutting mat. Place the ruler at a right angle on the edge of the fabric and trim off a small amount of fabric to make a straight edge. This starts to square up your fabric.

3 Lay out a strip. Line the edge of the fabric with the edge of the ruler and cut. The end of the fabric now has three perfect 90-degree angles. You can now cut off as many squares as you need, using the measuring line on the ruler for reference.

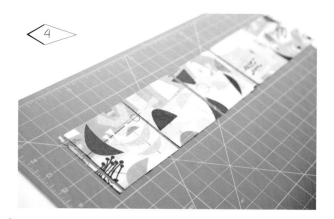

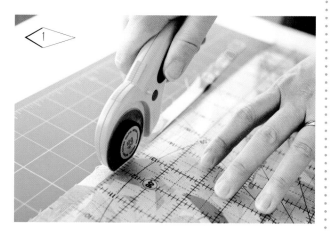

2 Turn the fabric round, and line up the 4in (10.2cm) line on your ruler with the straight edge of the fabric and cut a strip. Repeat to cut as many strips as required..

Safety tips

A rotary cutter is a circular blade. You need to take care with this tool as accidents can occur.

* **Every time you finish cutting, cover the blade immediately.**
* **Cut away from you in one movement.**
* **Always use your acrylic ruler; never be tempted to use a normal one.**
* **Be careful to ensure that your fingers are not over the edge of the ruler when you cut.**
* **If you feel the ruler slip when you cut, buy some sticky pads to apply to the ruler to keep it in place. You can also stop cutting halfway up a piece of fabric, move your hands up, then continue cutting.**
* **Take care when changing the blade on your cutter. It will need changing when it stops cutting correctly.**
* **Discard old blades carefully.**

Making a quilt sandwich

Once you have made your quilt top, the next stage is to make a quilt sandwich, so called as it has three layers – the backing, wadding (batting) and quilt top. As this is purely functional and not creative, it is my least favourite part of the quilt-making process, but it is essential to take time over it and get it right so you end up with a lovely, smooth quilt.

Sometimes it may be necessary to join pieces of fabric together to make a large enough piece of backing fabric. If you need to join two fabrics together, press the seams open so the fabric lies flat. It does not have to be the same fabric used – I really like the look of a quilt back which features more than one fabric. Alternatively, you can buy extra wide, craft-weight fabric.

Assembling the layers

1 Press the backing fabric, then lay it out on a table or floor, right side down. Smooth it out so it is flat. If I am working on a quilt larger than 1yd (1m), then it can be helpful to use low tack masking tape to secure the backing to a surface, which helps keep it flat while you work. Make sure it is not pulled too tight.

2 Lay the wadding (batting) on top. Smooth it so it is completely flat.

3 Take the quilt top, press it flat and snip off any loose threads.

4 Place the quilt top on the wadding (batting) and backing, ensuring it is positioned in the middle. I like to have an extra 4in (10.2cm) of wadding (batting) and backing on each side of my quilt top. This allows for any movement while quilting. Smooth again, so all three layers are flat.

5 Use quilter's safety pins to hold the layers together. Starting in the centre, pin every 4–6in (10.2–15.2cm) in rows, to make a grid format. Alternatively, you can tack (baste) large stitches across the quilt sandwich in a grid format.

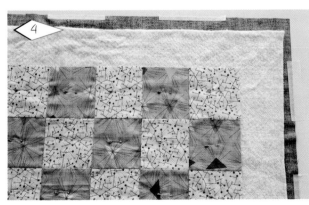

Quilting

Quilting is the process that holds the layers together. It is decorative, adding pattern and texture, but also functional – without quilting, the wadding (batting), which gives the quilt warmth, would ball up within the quilt after a few washes. Wholecloth quilts are made from a single piece of fabric that is quilted, which is a great way of using a favourite piece of fabric without piecing it. Give yourself time to ponder on whether you wish to hand or machine quilt, and what sort of design you wish to use. Look through books and go to quilt shows for ideas on how others have used quilting to enhance their quilts. For inspiration, look at the fabrics used in quilts – fabrics with circles may inspire curved quilting, and geometric shapes might suggest straight line quilting, or you can just quilt an allover pattern.

Whether you hand or machine quilt, always start in the middle and work your way out to the edges. This helps to smooth the layers as you work.

Marking the quilting pattern

You can stitch around the pieces of fabric, using your eye for guidance, but in most instances you will want to mark your quilting lines on the top. You can either mark your quilt up before assembling the layers, which is good as there are no pins to get in the way, or afterwards, which is handy if using a chalk marker as it rubs off easily and may otherwise disappear by the time you start quilting.

There are a wide variety of marking tools available. My favourites are:

Water-soluble pens: Draw your quilting shapes on the fabric then, when you have finished, the pen comes out when it comes into contact with water. Always test the pen on a piece of scrap fabric before using it on a quilt, and never iron as it fixes it.

Quilter's masking tape: This is ¼in (0.6cm) wide and low tack so it doesn't leave any residue on the fabric. You stick it on the quilt top, then stitch alongside it, being careful not to stitch on top of it. You can re-use masking tape in various places on the quilt until it loses its tack.

Chalk liners: These draw a line in chalk which can be easily removed. The white chalk is ideal for marking dark fabrics that are too dark to show a water-soluble marker. Always test on a scrap of fabric before use, especially if using yellow or blue chalk.

Tie or button quilting

The easiest way to quilt by hand is simply to tie lengths of perle or embroidery thead at regular intervals through your quilt. Starting in the middle of the quilt, with the right side facing, take the needle through to the back, then up again to the front about ¼in (0.6cm) away from the first stitch. Take the thread through to the back, then the front again and tie off in a reef knot. Trim to leave a tail, which can be as long as you wish. You can double thread your needle for more definition.

Button quilting works in the same way, with the buttons being sewn on through the quilt. They can look very decorative, especially if you choose interesting buttons that contrast with the fabric.

Hand quilting

Hand quilting is relaxing to do and, once you have got into a rhythm, surprisingly quick. I like to quilt in front of the television in the evenings. Big stitch quilting, also known as utilitarian quilting, is an easy way to learn the basics of hand quilting. It uses a big needle and chunky thread to make prominent stitches. I use a chenille needle, size 22 or 24, although you can also use embroidery needles; a size 5 is good. When you start, buy a pack of needles in mixed sizes and try a variety to see which one you are happy with. It is a must to wear a thimble, and again try a number of different types to find one that suits you. Finally, I like to use a frame when hand quilting. Plastic, tubular frames are good as they pull apart so are easy to store. Don't pull the fabric taut in the frame, and if there are any pins in the place where you want to put the fabric in the frame, remove them first.

How to big stitch quilt

1 Thread your needle with approximately 18in (45.7cm) of thread. Knot the end.

2 With the quilt top facing upwards, place the needle through the top and wadding (batting) 1in (2.5cm) away from where you want to start quilting. Make sure the needle only goes through the layers, not to the back. Pull the thread and then 'pop' the knot through the quilt top and wadding (batting) so it is secure and hidden inside the quilt. If the end of the thread has left a tail, trim it.

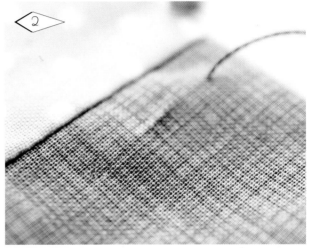

3 Now start making a row of stitches. Don't worry too much about what size your stitches are, but try to make them all the same size. A running stitch will give you large stitches on top, and smaller stitches on the back.

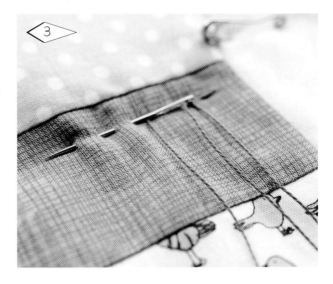

If you want even stitches on the back and front of your quilt, place the needle through the quilt vertically from the top. Have your other hand under the quilt to feel when the needle comes through. Move the needle along to make the stitch underneath, then use your finger to guide the needle back up vertically.

4 When the thread on your needle starts to run out, or you get to the end of a particular area of stitching, whichever comes first, make a knot in your thread one stitch length away from the quilt top. Make your last stitch by travelling at least 1in (2.5cm) through the quilt top and wadding (batting), not to the back, and 'pop' the thread through the layers again. Trim any excess thread.

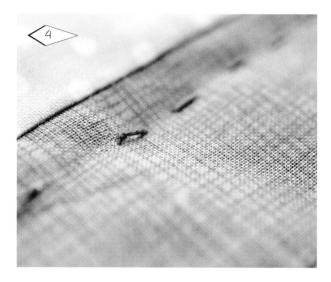

When quilting, you might like to load two or three stitches on to your needle at a time, then pull the thread through, but this is not essential.

Straight stitch machine quilting

Machine quilting is much quicker than hand quilting. However, take time to ensure your machine is set up properly as unpicking machine quilting is a long and thankless task! You may find it easier to practise on smaller pieces of work first, such as cushion covers, then work up to a large quilt. Another tip is to stitch straight lines across the quilt as the binding hides where you stopped and started, and you don't need to trim the ends of the thread. A walking foot (also known as an even feed foot) is essential for straight stitch machine quilting. The foot has a set of feed dogs in it so the three layers are fed through the machine evenly. I use a quilting needle, size 75/12, in my machine, as it is sharp, and thread made for machine quilting, as it is stronger. If you are working on a larger quilt, roll the areas of your quilt that are not being sewn to help it fit through your machine.

How to straight stitch machine quilt

1 Following the manufacturer's instructions, fit the walking foot to your sewing machine. Thread the machine with machine quilting thread then set the stitch length to your machine's shortest setting.

2 Position the quilt under the foot of your sewing machine at the starting point. Hold on to the thread from the needle and lower then raise the needle. When the needle is raised, pull on the thread and this will bring the bobbin thread through.

3 Hold the threads to the back and sew about five stitches to secure the thread. Stop, change the stitch length to 3, then start quilting your design. If you need to change direction, make sure the needle is down, lift the presser foot and pivot your quilt. This ensures that your stitching looks continuous. Remove any pins that get in the way of the foot as you go.

4 When you get to the end of your stitching, stop with the needle down. Set the stitch length back to its shortest setting and make four or five stitches to secure. Take the quilt out from the machine and trim the threads.

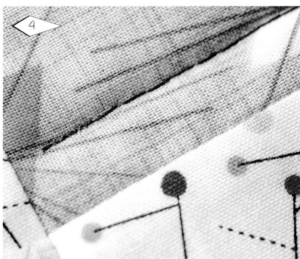

Binding

Binding means finishing the edges, and it is the last stage of making a quilt. Here are my two favourite, easy techniques for binding.

Self binding

In this method you bring the backing round to the front of the quilt to encase the edges. I find this the easiest way to bind a quilt and, as you don't need to cut any extra fabric, it is also economical. When using this technique, make sure you use a backing that will look good when it comes round to the front of the quilt.

1 When you have finished quilting, use scissors to cut the wadding (batting) so it is level with the front of the quilt. Then cut the backing 1½in (3.8cm) wider than the quilt all the way round; if you wish to have a narrower binding, cut the backing 1in (2.5cm) wider. A useful tip is to place your acrylic ruler between the wadding (batting) and backing when cutting so you are not likely to snip into the backing fabric.

2 Lay the quilt right side up. On the two opposite sides fold the raw edge of the backing to the edge of the quilt, then press. Then fold the backing again over the front of the quilt to make a hem.

Press and use pins or binding clips (they look like click-clack hair grips) to hold the binding in place. Slipstitch the hem using thread that tones with the binding, taking care only to sew through the quilt top and wadding (batting). Repeat with the top and bottom.

3 I often quilt another line around the edge of the quilt after it is bound, ½in (0.6cm) away from the edge of the binding. This helps the edge to stay crisp.

Mitred double fold binding

This method uses a strip of fabric which is sewn to the front of the quilt. When planning fabric for this type of binding, take into consideration that only a small strip will be seen. Small prints work well, striped fabric can be fun, and don't be afraid to use a contrasting colour as it acts as a frame. The two layers of fabric in the binding give the quilt a strong edge.

1 When the quilting is complete, cut the wadding (batting) and backing level with the edge of the quilt top.

2 Work out the length of the binding you need to make, by adding together the measurements of each side of the quilt, then adding an extra 10in (25.4cm). From your binding fabric, cut strips 2½in (6.3cm) wide.

3 Join the strips together at a 45-degree angle. Draw a 45-degree line on the wrong side of one of the strips. Line it up at a 90-degree angle on top of another strip, right sides together. Stitch along the line, trim the seam allowance to ¼in (0.6cm) and press the seams open.

4 Fold the binding in half, wrong side together, and press.

5 Fold under a ½in (1.3cm) hem at one end of the binding and press.

6 Starting on one side of the quilt, pin the binding to the front with the raw edges together. Start one-third of the way along one side, leaving a tail of binding 2½in (6.3cm) long, from the end that has had the raw edge turned in. Using a walking foot on your sewing machine, sew the binding to the quilt front, using a ⅜in (0.9cm) seam allowance. It helps to pin the binding in place as you sew each side, removing the pins as they get to the edge of the walking foot. When you reach the end of the side, stop sewing ⅜in (0.9cm) before the edge, and backstitch to secure. Take the quilt from the machine, fold the binding up away from the quilt top, then fold back down.

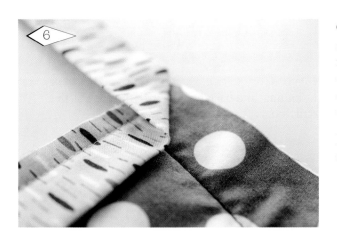

Pin to secure. Start sewing from the corner, with a ⅜in (0.9cm) seam allowance. Repeat at the other three corners.

7 When you get to 4in (10.2cm) before your starting point, stop sewing. Tuck the end of the binding in the folded end. Trim the excess binding 1in (2.5cm) beyond the hem so it overlaps. Pin and finish sewing.

8 Turn the quilt over, fold the binding to the back and slipstitch, covering the line of machine sewing. At the corners, fold the mitre in on the back so it looks the same as the front and secure with a couple of stitches. If you want a ¼in (0.6cm) wide binding, cut your strips to 2¼in (5.7cm), then sew with a ¼in (0.6cm) seam allowance.

Play around with different combinations of width and seam allowance.

Labelling

Label your finished quilt with the maker's name, the date, who the quilt was made for and the quilt title. You can do this by writing on a piece of cotton fabric with a permanent fabric pen and then stitching it to the quilt back. Alternatively, you can embroider the details on a piece of fabric then stitch this to the back of the quilt.

Projects

Patchwork Rosette Needle Book

Every respectable sewing box should have a handmade needle book! This project is straightforward to make and uses only small pieces of fabric and felt. The hexagon rosette on the front is made using the English paper piecing technique, where the fabric is tacked (basted) over paper templates before the shapes are sewn together. I am a huge fan of this technique as it is portable; I take a small tin of work along with me when waiting to collect my children from their after-school activities. You can make larger pieces of patchwork using this technique but it can be time-consuming, so this small project is a good way to try it out before committing to making a quilt. English paper piecing should come with a warning though, as it is addictive!

FINISHED SIZE: 5in x 4½in (12.7cm x 11.4cm)

• Get

* 4¼in x 4¼in (10.8cm x 10.8cm) felt for the rosette backing
* 5in x 9½in (12.7cm x 24.1cm) felt for the needle book cover
* 4½in x 9in (11.4cm x 24.1cm) felt for the inside page of the needle book
* 7 pieces of fabric, a minimum of 2¼in (5.7cm) square
* 100% cotton thread for tacking (basting) and piecing
* Perle thread, no 8
* Pinking shears (optional)
* Scissors, for paper and fabric
* Ruler and pencil
* A4 paper, photocopy weight
* Glue stick
* 4in (10.2cm) square of card
* Pins
* Sharps sewing needle
* Iron
* Chenille needle

•• Ready

* If you have bought large pieces of felt, cut them down to size now. I cut the two rectangular shapes with pinking shears. If you don't have any, cut them straight-edged with normal scissors.
* To make the hexagon template, trace the shape (see page 120) on to paper. Trim, leaving a border approximately ½in (1.3cm) from the line, then stick the shape on to card. Cut out the shape along the line. Place the template on your paper, and cut out seven shapes using scissors.

••• Sew

1 Pin one of the paper hexagons to the wrong side of a piece of fabric and cut the fabric round the paper shape, leaving a ¼in (0.6cm) seam allowance. Repeat with each hexagon, using whatever fabric you wish.

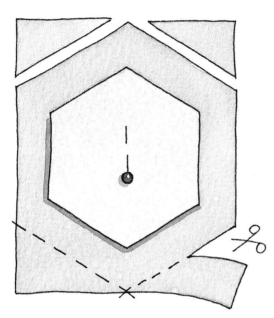

2 Pick up one of the shapes and fold the excess fabric to the back. Thread a needle and tie a knot in the end. Fold the excess fabric over the paper, then sew through the paper and fabric, folding the corners as you go. When you come to the end of the stitching, sew a single backstitch. Repeat this with each hexagon.

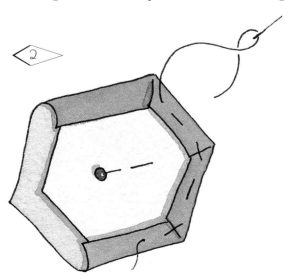

3 Lay out your hexagons and, once they are in an order you are happy with, pick up the central one and one of the border ones. Place their right sides together. Using a colour thread that tones with the project, thread a needle. Start stitching ¼in (0.6cm) in from the right end, holding the end of the thread; oversew a few stitches to the beginning, then stitch along the seam, sewing back by ¼in (0.6cm) at the end. This acts like a backstitch to secure the stitching. Sew the other five hexagons on to the central hexagon in the same way.

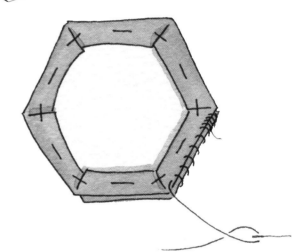

4 Sew up between the rows using the same method.

5 Press the rosette with a medium hot iron (so you don't scorch the paper). Then carefully unpick the tacking (basting) stitches and take the paper out. Don't throw the paper away as it can be re-used.

6 Place the hexagons in the centre of the felt square and pin into place. Slipstitch around the rosette using a toning thread. Don't worry too much about your stitching on the back – it will not be seen.

7 Fold the felt for the needle book cover in half and press the fold with your finger to help hold it in place. Place the felt-backed rosette on the front in the centre. Using the perle thread and a chenille needle, sew a running stitch around the edge of the felt square. I started using a knot, which I hid in the layers, then finished with a backstitch, also hidden between the layers of fabric.

8 Draw a line in pencil down the centre of the felt to be used for the inside of the needle book. Lay the outside of the book right side down and place the inner page in the centre. When you are happy it is in place, pin to secure then, using perle thread, sew up the line with running stitch. Fold the book in half and finger press down the fold. It is now ready to use.

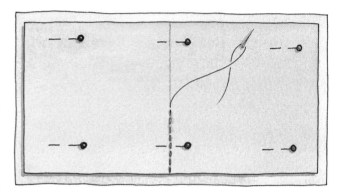

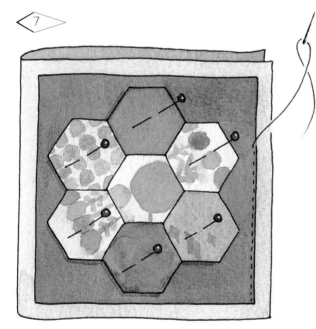

Take it further...
Draw up a bigger hexagon
template and use the rosette to
go in the centre of a cushion

Flowered Dolly's Quilt

Pretty Liberty fabrics have been used to make this doll quilt which was sewn by hand – yes, all of it! I am a huge fan of hand sewing; although it takes longer than using a sewing machine, you can work on it anywhere. If you don't know of a doll in need of a quilt, it also looks lovely hung on a wall.

The edge of the quilt is finished using a "bagging" technique, which works well for small items. In this technique you sew around the edge of the quilt with the right sides facing in, then leave a small gap to turn it inside out – if you think of the method of putting on a duvet cover you are on the right lines!

FINISHED SIZE: 18in x 22½in (45.7cm x 57.1cm)

• Get

✽ A4 sheet of template plastic or card
✽ Fabric grips to stick on the back of template plastic, optional
✽ 5 metric fat eighths (25cm x 55cm) in complementary colours
✽ 100% cotton thread for piecing
✽ 18½in x 23in (47cm x 58.4cm) wadding (batting)
✽ 19½in x 23in (49.5cm x 58.4cm) cotton fabric for quilt backing
✽ Perle thread, no 8, for quilting (I used 2 colours)
✽ Fine permanent marker or pencil for writing on template plastic
✽ Ruler and pencil
✽ Scissors, for paper and fabric
✽ Fabric marking pen or pencil (I use a Sewline pen)
✽ Quilter's ruler with inch markings or a ¼in (0.6cm) seamer
✽ Pins
✽ Sharps sewing needle
✽ Chenille needle

•• Ready

✽ Make your templates from template plastic or card. Template plastic is stronger, but you can use card, then replace it if it becomes damaged. Draw your shape on to the plastic with a fine permanent pen or pencil. You will need two templates, a rectangle measuring 4½in x 2½in (11.4cm x 6.3cm) and a square measuring 2½in x 2½in (6.3cm x 6.3cm). Cut out the shapes. If desired, you can stick fabric grips on the back of the templates. These are small stickers with a rough surface, which help to stop the template slipping.

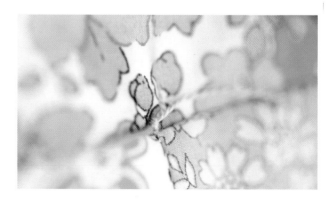

··· Sew

1 Lay out one of the fat eighths of fabric, right side down. Place the rectangular template on the fabric and draw around it using a fabric marking pen or pencil. Next, using a quilter's ruler or ¼in (0.6cm) seamer, draw another line ¼in (0.6cm) away from the first line, all the way round. Cut out the shape using fabric scissors, following the outside line. Cut out four rectangles from each piece of fabric.

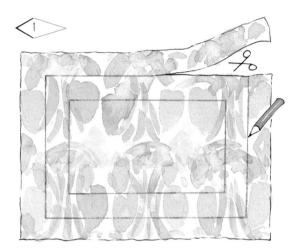

2 Using the square template, follow the same technique to mark up and cut out one square from each piece of fabric.

Take it further...

To make a bigger quilt, simply scale up the templates. Finish off the edges with binding.

3 Lay out four fabric rectangles in the order you wish to have for your top row. Place the first two rectangles on top of each other with right sides together. On the side to be joined, place a pin through the marked pencil line in the corner, making sure it goes through both layers of fabric. Do the same at the other corner. Make sure both pieces of fabric are lined up. Place another pin through the line halfway along the seam to hold the fabric in place.

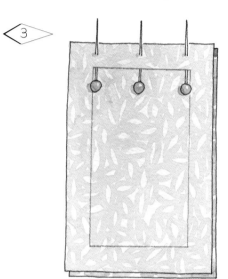

4 Now sew a running stitch along the marked seam to join the two rectangles together, taking care to follow the pencil line on both sides. It helps to keep looking on the back to check the stitching. Start with a knot, and finish with a backstitch. Using the same technique, sew the other two fabric rectangles together. Next, join the two sets, then you have your first row.

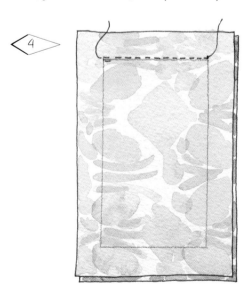

5 Carry on sewing the fabric together to make rows in the same way, cutting out more fabric rectangles as you need them. You need to make five rows of four rectangles, and four rows of three rectangles and a square at each end.

6 Press the rows with the seams together, facing the direction of the darkest piece of fabric.

7 Place the first and second row together, right sides facing, and put a pin through each end, in the same way as for sewing the patches together. Place more pins along the row to line up the seam. Sew along the seam using a running stitch. When you get to a seam intersection, take the needle through the seam allowance but don't sew it down. Secure each end with a couple of backstitches, then keep adding on the rows.

8 Press the patchwork, making sure the seams are pressed together, not open. Place the wadding (batting) on a table and smooth it flat. Lay the backing fabric on top, right side up, then the patchwork on top right side down. Smooth out and pin the layers together. Using backstitch, sew round the edge, following the pencil line on the sides of the patchwork for guidance. Start 4in (10.1cm) up from the bottom on one side, and finish 6in (15.2cm) before this. Clip the corners and turn out, gently easing out the corners. Slipstitch the opening to close.

9 The doll quilt is quilted using the method of tie quilting. You can sew as many ties as you like, but make sure the quilt is covered enough to hold it together, particularly if it is going to be played with. To make a tie, thread a needle with a piece of perle thread approximately 24in (60.9cm) long, doubling it up so the needle is in the middle of the thread. From the front, put the needle through the quilt to the back, making sure you leave a 4in (10.1cm) tail on the front. Bring the needle back up to the front close to where you started. Take another stitch – from the front to the back and up again. Now, using the tail left at the beginning, tie a reef knot – left over right then right over left. I have trimmed the tails to 1in (2.5cm), but you can leave as much as you like.

9

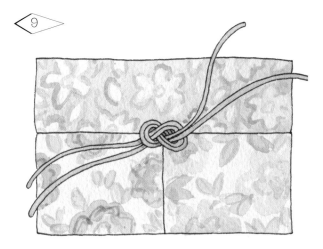

8

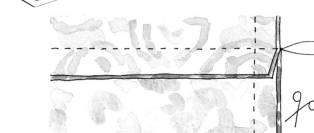

Tote-ally Fabulous Bag

The appliqué pattern on this bag was inspired by some of the fabulous 1950s prints from the Festival of Britain. I chose the cross-hatch fabric to fit in with the era as it reminded me of the top of vintage Formica tables.

The method of appliqué used in this project is really straightforward, with the raw edges tacked (basted) under the pieces before they are slipstitched to the backing fabric. The bag is quilted, which gives it body, and it has a thick, comfortable handle. The size is handy to use either for shopping or as a workbag – it holds an A4 pad, sandwich and drink quite easily.

FINISHED SIZE: 16in x 13¼in (40.6cm x 33.6cm) excluding handles

• Get

* 4in (10.2cm) square of template plastic or card
* 20in (0.5m) fabric for outside of bag
* 20in (0.5m) fabric for lining
* 3 fat eighths for appliqué
* Thread for making bag
* 2 pieces of 18in x 21in (45.7cm x 53.3cm) thin calico for backing
* Thread for appliqué, to tone with fat eighths
* 2 pieces of 18in x 21in (45.7cm x 53.3cm) wadding (batting)
* Perle thread, no 8, for quilting
* Pencil
* Scissors
* Disappearing fabric pen
* Sharps sewing needle
* Pins
* Quilter's safety pins
* ¼in (0.6cm) wide low-tack masking tape
* Chenille sewing needle
* Sewing machine, ¼in (0.6cm) foot and zigzag foot
* Iron

•• Ready

* Trace the template on to a piece of template plastic or card. Cut out.
* Take the fabric for the outside of the bag and cut: two pieces measuring 16½in x 14in (41.9cm x 35.6cm), and two pieces measuring 3in x 16½in (7.6cm x 41.9cm).
* Take the fabric for the lining and cut two pieces measuring 16½in x 14in (41.9cm x 35.6cm), and two pieces measuring 3in x 16½in (7.6cm x 41.9cm).
* The 3in x 16½in (7.6cm x 41.9cm) pieces are for the handles; put to one side.

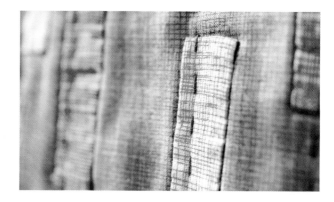

••• Sew

1 Prepare your appliqué pieces. Lay out one of the fat eighths and draw around the template on the front of the fabric using a disappearing fabric pen.

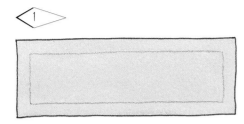

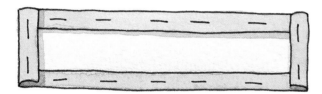

Use scissors to cut the fabric ¼in (0.6cm) away from this line. Using the pen line as a guide, finger press the excess fabric behind the shape. Tack (baste) the hem down using a needle and thread.

Note that the disappearing fabric pen can fade very quickly, so only mark one at a time. Make ten of these from each of your three fabrics.

2 Lay out both pieces of backing fabric, then place the appliqué pieces on top. Ensure you have an equal number on each piece of backing fabric, and that they are not near the edge. When you are happy with the arrangement, pin them in place. Slipstitch them on to the backing fabric. Try to use thread that tones with the colour of the piece you are sewing on to the backing.

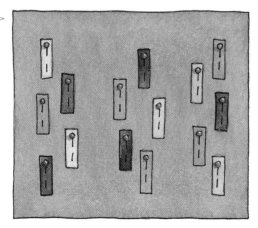

3 Assemble the quilt sandwich for each bag panel. Lay down the calico, then place the wadding (batting) on top and smooth. Finally, place the bag panel in the centre, then smooth. Use quilter's safety pins to hold the layers together. Place pins in a grid format across the fabric.

4 Quilt the bag panels. I hand quilted vertical lines at a slight angle. Mark your quilting line with low-tack masking tape, then quilt next to it (never stitch through it).

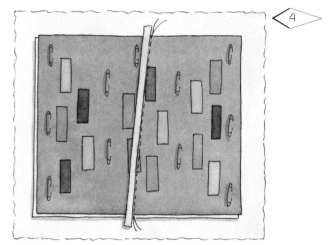

As the back is not going to be seen, I started with a knot on the back and finished with a backstitch, making sure the knots were in line with the back of the bag fabric. When you have finished quilting, trim the wadding (batting) and backing level with the front of the bag.

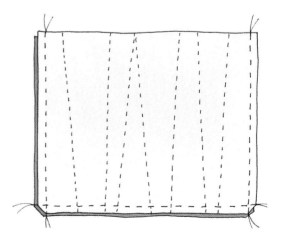

5 Place the bag panels right sides together, and stitch the sides and bottom ¼in (0.6cm) away from the edge. Clip the corners and turn inside out.

6 Make the handles. Take a piece of each colour, lay them right sides together and sew down each side, ¼in (0.6cm) away from the edge of the fabric. Turn inside out and press. Stich another line ¼in (0.6cm) away from the edge and press again.

7 Lay the handles on the bag, 3½in (8.9cm) away from each edge and pin to secure. Machine stitch several times very close to the edge to hold them in place. Remove the pins.

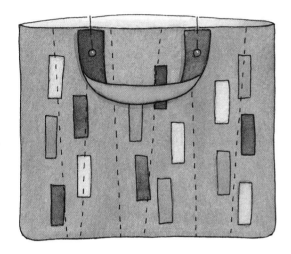

8 Place the lining pieces right sides together. Taking a ¼in (0.6cm) seam allowance, stitch the sides, then sew the bottom leaving an 8½in (21.6cm) gap open in the middle.

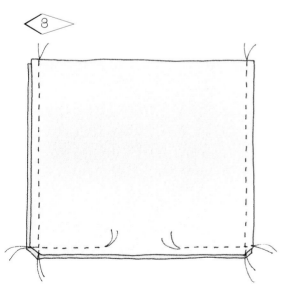

9 Place the bag inside the lining, right sides together, with the bag handles inside.

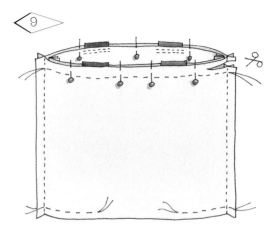

Pin, then sew around the top with a ½in (1.3cm) seam allowance. Using scissors, trim the seam allowance back to a scant ¼in (0.6cm). Turn the bag through the hole left in the bottom of the lining. Use your fingers to press the top seam.

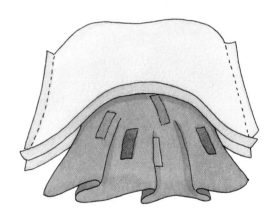

10 Set the sewing machine stitch length to 3. Start ¼in (0.6cm) in from one side and topstitch ¼in (0.6cm) from the top.

11 Stitch up the hole in the lining.

Take it further...
Use the pattern to make a version with plain fabric, or appliqué your own motif on it.

Simple Seedheads Table Mat

The colours of this quilted table mat have been chosen to fit in with my interior. Placed on the centre of my dining table, it looks perfect with a 1970s stoneware vase on top! This simple project is ideal for a beginner to try hand quilting – it is not as scary as being presented with a huge quilt to stitch. You don't need a sewing machine to make this, and the pieces can be cut out with scissors. Traditional hand quilting uses finer thread and a small needle, but this project uses perle thread for quilting so it is quicker to sew.

FINISHED SIZE: 15in x 12in (38.1cm x 30.5cm)

• Get

❋ 15in x 12in (38.1cm x 30.5cm) plain fabric
❋ 21in x 18in (53.3cm x 45.7cm) patterned fabric, for backing
❋ 21in x 18in (53.3cm x 45.7cm) wadding (batting)
❋ Perle thread, no 8, for quilting
❋ Thread for sewing binding
❋ Scissors
❋ Water-soluble fabric pen
❋ Quilter's safety pins
❋ Chenille needle
❋ Kitchen paper
❋ Iron
❋ Sharps sewing needle
❋ Pins
❋ ¼in (0.6cm) wide low-tack masking tape

• • Ready

❋ If you have not already done so, cut the plain fabric to 15in x 12in (38.1cm x 30.5cm) and the patterned fabric to 21in x 18in (53.3cm x 45.7cm).

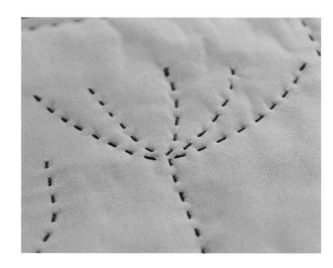

••• Sew

1 Trace the motifs (see Templates, page 118) on to the plain fabric using a water-soluble pen. If you find it tricky to see the lines through the fabric, use a light box. Alternatively, copy the pattern on to paper, then tape this up at a window. Tape the fabric on top, and then trace the motifs.

2 Lay out the backing on a table, right side down, and place the wadding (batting) in the centre and smooth. Finally, put the plain fabric on top in the middle and smooth. There should be approximately 3in (7.6cm) extra for each side. Use quilter's safety pins to hold the layers together, placing them across the fabric about 4in (10.2cm) apart, in a grid format.

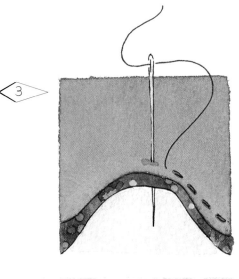

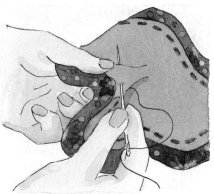

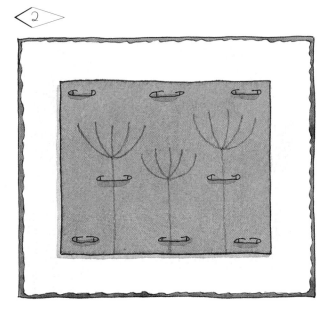

3 To start quilting, thread a chenille needle with approximately 18in (45.7cm) of perle thread. Knot the end.

When quilting, to achieve a good, even stitch through the layers, push the needle through the fabric from the front at a 90-degree angle. Take the needle one stitch length along the back, then use your finger underneath the fabric to push the needle back through to the front at a 90-degree angle. This helps to give you an even-sized stitch on the front and back.

Alternatively, sew a standard running stitch. This gives you smaller stitches on the back but is much quicker to do. Start the quilting at the centre motif, placing the knot between the layers at the bottom of the stem. Sew up the stem following the line. When you get to the top of the stem, continue quilting up the left-hand side of the motif. Stop one stitch before the end and make a knot in the thread one stitch length from the end. Take the last stitch and pop the knot through, taking care only to go through the top fabric and wadding (batting). Take the needle through the layers about 1in (2.5cm) then come back up to the front. Snip the thread.

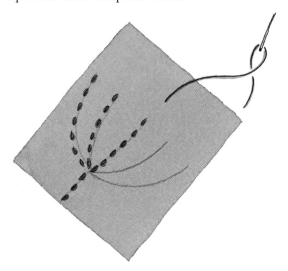

4 Make a knot in the end of the thread. Push the needle through the top layer and wadding (batting) 1in (2.5cm) away from the end of the second to left line of the motif. Bring the needle back up to the front at the end of the second to left motif. Pop the knot. Continue quilting down that line, then back up the next one.

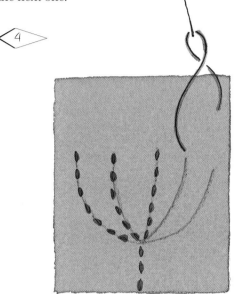

When you get back to the top, stop one stitch length before the end and finish the thread as before.

5 Sew the two lines on the right-hand side of the central motif in the same way.

6 Repeat steps 3 to 5 to sew the other two motifs in the same way.

7 Make the water-soluble marker disappear by wetting a piece of kitchen paper with cold water, then dabbing it lightly on top of the fabric. (Never apply heat to water-soluble marker as it can fix it.)

8 Cut the wadding (batting) level with the top fabric. Cut the backing so it is 1½in (3.8cm) wider than the centre fabric all the way round.

Take it further...
Draw your own motif,
then trace and stitch.

9 At the sides, fold the raw edges of the backing in so they are level with the raw edges of the wadding (batting). Press, then fold over again to make a hem around the quilt and press again. Pin, then slipstitch in place using thread for binding. Fold the top and bottom edges over in the same way, and slipstitch to secure.

10 Quilt a further line ¼in (0.6cm) away from the edge of the binding. Stop and start the quilting using the method in step 4. You can either quilt the line for the border by eye, or place a piece of ¼in (0.6cm) wide masking tape next to the edge of the binding then quilt next to this line.

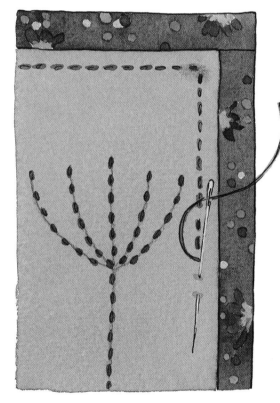

Checkerboard Charms Car Quilt

Car quilts are so useful. Comforting and warm on long winter drives, they are also handy to use as a picnic blanket in summer. Take inspiration for your choice of fabric from the colour of the car it is being made for. Whether it is a cool, vintage camper van, or a shabby run-around, a co-ordinating quilt can make a car look and feel loved. This project is a good introduction to machine piecing. It uses two Charm Packs, one plain, one printed. A Charm Pack is a bundle of 42 co-ordinating pre-cut 5in (12.7cm) squares. You can buy them in a variety of styles, from zingy, graphic brights to more muted florals, and they also come in packs of plain fabrics. As you don't need to cut the squares yourself, it speeds up the making process.

FINISHED SIZE: 45½in x 36½in (115.6cm x 92.7cm)

• Get

* 1 patterned Charm Pack (or 40 x 5in (12.7cm) squares)
* 1 plain Charm Pack (or 40 x 5in (12.7cm) squares)
* Thread for piecing
* 10g ball perle cotton, no 8, for quilting
* Thread for binding, to tone with backing
* 44in x 55in (110cm x 140cm) backing fabric
* 44in x 55in (110cm x 140cm) wadding (batting)
* Rotary cutter, acrylic ruler and self-healing mat (optional)
* Sewing machine and ¼in (0.6cm) foot
* Iron
* Pins
* Quilter's safety pins
* Quilt marking tool (I used a Chaco Liner) and ruler
* Tubular quilting frame (optional)
* Chenille needle
* Scissors
* Binding clips (optional)
* Sharps sewing needle

•• Ready

* Cut out your fabric squares with a rotary cutter and self-healing mat if not using Charm Packs. Lay out the charm squares, ten squares across, eight rows down, alternating patterned and plain squares.

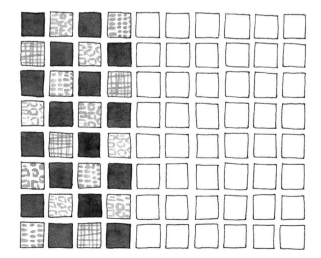

••• Sew

1 Take the first two squares from the top row and line them up, right sides together. Sew together using a ¼in (0.6cm) seam allowance. Then pick up the next square, line up and sew. Repeat until you have all ten rows sewn together.

2 Place the top row on an ironing board, right side down. Press the seams together with them facing the same way. Then turn the row over and give it another press from the front. Iron the second row in the same way, but this time press the seams together in the opposite direction.

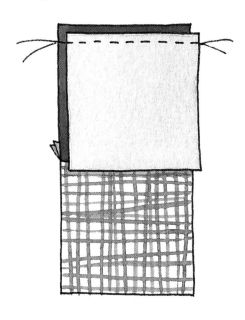

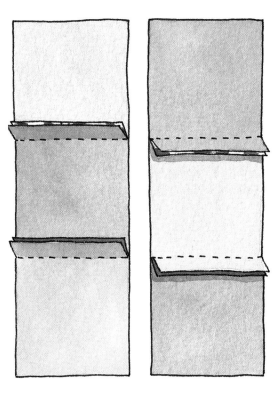

3 Place the two rows on top of each other with right sides together. Line up the squares and you will see that where the seams have been pressed in different directions, they lock together.

Pinch the seam allowances to make sure the seams are nestled in, then insert a pin through the fabric to hold them in place. Repeat at each seam along the row of squares.

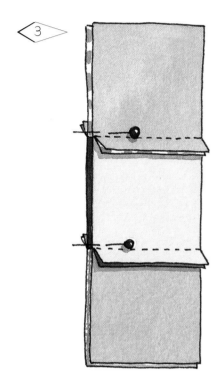

Taking a ¼in (0.6cm) seam allowance, sew along this row, taking the pins out as they go under the foot, so you don't stitch over them.

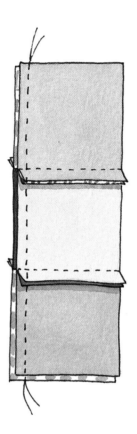

Use the same technique to join the rest of the rows, taking care to press the seams on each row in alternate directions. Once the rows are sewn together, press the quilt top.

4 Lay out the backing fabric, right side down. Smooth it out so it is flat. Lay the wadding (batting) on top and smooth it flat. Place the quilt top on the wadding (batting) and backing, ensuring it is positioned in the middle. Smooth again, so all three layers are flat. Use quilter's safety pins to hold the layers together. Starting in the centre, pin every 4in–6in (10.2cm–15.2cm) in rows in a grid format.

5 Starting with a square in the centre of the quilt, use a chalk liner and a ruler to mark the quilting line ¾in (1.9cm) inside the edge. As I was using a chalk liner, I marked a square at a time in case the line rubbed off. If you like, place the fabric in a tubular quilting frame to quilt.

6 Thread a chenille needle with approximately 18in (45.7cm) of thread. Tie a knot in the end, then place the needle through the quilt top and wadding (batting) but not the backing, about 1in (2.5cm) away from where you want to start quilting. Gently pull the thread till you 'pop' the knot through the layers. Give a gentle pull to make sure the thread is secure, then start quilting. When you get towards the end of the marked

⟨ 5 ⟩

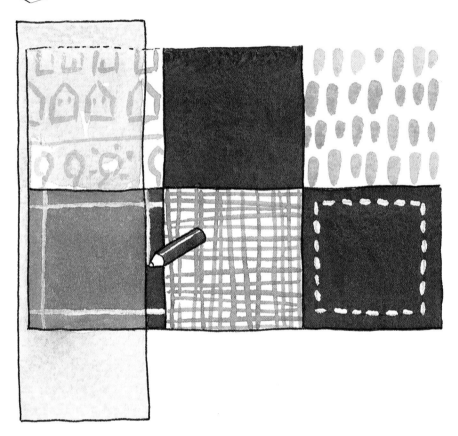

section, stop one stitch before the end. Tie a knot in the thread, one stitch length away from the quilt top, then make the last stitch, putting the needle just through the top and wadding (batting), bringing the needle back out 1in (2.5cm) away. Pull so the knot pops and is secured in the layers. When you take this last stitch, push the needle through the layer, travelling about 1in (2.5cm). Trim the thread.

Keep quilting the plain squares, working methodically from the centre outwards. When you quilt the squares at the edge, you can just start at the side and hide the knot in the layers, rather than popping it though the top.

7 Cut the wadding (batting) so it is level with the front of the quilt. Then cut the backing 1½in (3.8cm) wider than the quilt all the way around.

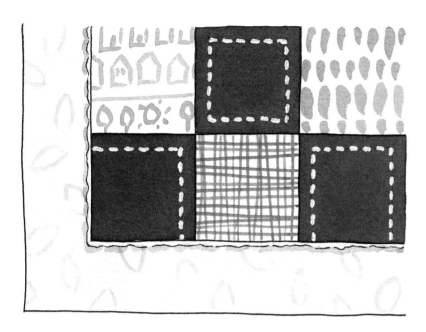

On the two opposite sides, fold the raw edge of the backing to the edge of the quilt, then press.

Then fold the backing again over the front of the quilt, and you will see you have made a hem. Press and use pins or binding clips to hold the binding in place. Slipstitch the hem using thread that tones with the binding, taking care only to sew through the quilt top and wadding (batting). Repeat the process with the top and bottom.

Take it further...
You could make a narrower, but longer, version of this quilt for an easy bed runner.

Summer Delight Table Runner

Gingham and vintage-patterned florals have been used to make this summery, retro table runner. The inspiration for my example is the large table in my parents' garden. Runners can also be brought indoors to smarten up tables, sideboards or beds. Table runners have increased in popularity over the last few years, and are particularly good to make for occasions such as Christmas and Hallowe'en, when seasonal fabrics are available, and they are a quick way of adding decoration to the house.

FINISHED SIZE: 76¾in x 15½in (195cm x 39.4cm)

• Get

* 3 x gingham fat quarters
* 3 x floral fat quarters
* Thread for piecing
* 40in x 44in (1m x 110cm) 100% cotton fabric for backing
* 20in x 79in (50cm x 2m) wadding (batting)
* Machine quilting thread
* Thread for binding (to tone with backing)
* Rotary cutter, acrylic ruler and self-healing mat
* Sewing machine, ¼in (0.6cm) foot and walking foot
* Iron
* Low-tack masking tape
* Quilter's safety pins
* Scissors
* Binding clips (optional)
* Sharps sewing needle

•• Ready

* Using a rotary cutter, ruler and self-healing mat (see page 21), cut the width of each fat quarter to 15½in (39.4cm), then from them cut the following strips, 3½in (8.9cm) wide: three strips of yellow gingham; two strips of yellow floral; four strips of red gingham; six strips of red floral; six strips of blue gingham; four strips of blue floral.

• • • Sew

1 The runner is made in five sections, which are then sewn together.

Start by sewing the two red sections. Lay a red floral strip on the table, then a gingham strip on either side. Then lay another floral strip on either side of these. Using a ¼in (0.6cm) seam allowance, sew the strips together.

2 Once the five sections are sewn together, press with the seams together. I pressed with the seams facing away from the gingham strips, but it does not matter which direction they go, just that the piece is pressed well.

3 Next, make two blue sections. Lay out the fabric strips as before, but this time place a gingham strip in the middle, with a floral strip on either side, then another gingham strip at each end. Sew and press as before.

4 Make one yellow section for the middle of the runner. Sew the yellow strips together, with a gingham strip in the middle, a floral strip on either side, then another gingham strip at each end. Sew and press as before.

5 Lay out the middle yellow piece on a table, then place the red sections on each side, making sure you change the direction the strips face. Next, lay out the two blue sections, changing the direction again.

6 Using a ¼in (0.6cm) seam, sew the sections together. Press with the seams together and trim any stray threads.

7 Take the backing fabric and cut through the centre fold, so you end up with two pieces of fabric measuring 40in x 21.6cm (1m x 55cm). Trim the selvedge off the ends then sew together using a ¼in (0.6cm) seam allowance. Press the seams open.

8 Place the backing on a table or floor, right side down. Tape the edges, ensuring the fabric is not pulled too tight. Lay the wadding (batting) on top and smooth the layers. Place the quilt top on the wadding (batting) and backing, positioning it in the middle. Smooth again, then use quilter's safety pins to hold the layers together. Starting in the centre, pin every 4–6in (10.2–15.2cm) in rows, to make a grid format.

9 Set up the machine for machine quilting. Fill the bobbin with the machine quilting thread and attach the walking foot. Quilt the centre panel first, then the middle panels, then the ends. I quilted straight lines, using the edge of the foot against the seam edge.

Start the quilting ¼in (0.6cm) in from the edge. Place the runner in the correct position to start, and lower the presser foot. Hold the thread through the needle, then lower the needle through the work, and bring it up again. Gently pull the piece of thread and this should bring the bobbin thread through to the front. Hold the threads out of the way, set the length on the sewing machine to its minimum setting and take about five stitches. Then reset the length to

3 and start quilting. When you get to the end, repeat how you started, taking a couple of small stitches to secure before cutting the threads.Keep quilting lines across each section of the runner until you are happy with the result. I quilted four lines across each section, each time using the edge of the foot against the edge of the fabric for guidance.

Alternate the side you start quilting from as this will help keep the runner straight. If any quilter's safety pins get in the way of your sewing, take them out as you stitch.

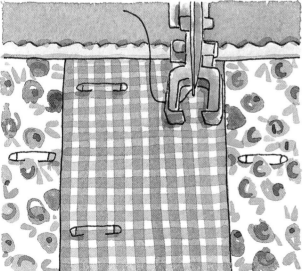

10 When the quilting is finished, remove all the quilter's safety pins. Then, using scissors, carefully trim the wadding (batting), but not the backing, so it is the same size as the patchwork top.

12 On the long side, fold the raw edge of the backing fabric to the edge of the patchwork and wadding (batting), then iron the fold.

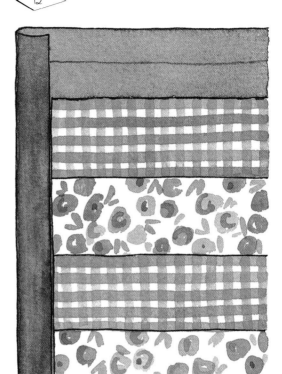

11 Using a rotary cutter, acrylic ruler and self-healing mat, trim the backing so it is 1½in (3.8cm) wider than the quilt top all the way round.

Take it further...
Make more strip sections in the same way, alternating the direction of the strips, and sew the rows together to create a large quilt.

Fold over again and carefully press the fold. Secure the hem down with binding clips.

13 Using a Sharps sewing needle and thread that tones with the backing fabric, slipstitch the fold down, ensuring that you only sew through the top and wadding (batting), not through to the back. Then bind the ends of the runner in the same way, folding in the corners so no raw edges are showing.

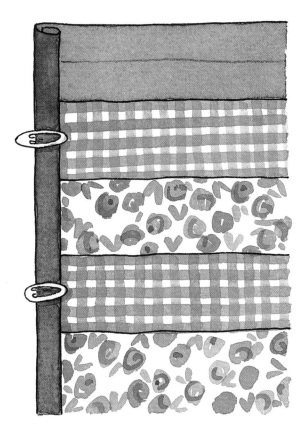

Spinning Around Cushion

There is something about circles that makes me think of 1960s' space exploration. I wanted to have fun with this cushion cover so I mixed up the fabrics and circle sizes to make the design look quirky, then completed the look with unusual binding.

The circles are fixed to the backing fabric using fusible web and the edges are secured by sewing a zigzag stitch. This is sewn once the cushion front is backed with wadding (batting), which means it also quilts the cushion front. You can have some fun and put your own stamp on the design by deciding how many fabrics you wish to use, and how many different-sized circles you would like.

FINISHED SIZE: 18in (45.7cm) square

• Get

* 19in x 19in (48.3cm x 48.3cm) fabric for the front
* 4 cotton fat quarters for the circles and binding
* 21in x 21in (53.3cm x 53.3cm) backing for the front
* 2 pieces of 19in by 15in (48.3cm x 38.1cm) cotton fabric for back
* 21in x 21in (53.3cm x 53.3cm) wadding (batting)
* 2 pieces of A4 card or template plastic
* 1 small pack of fusible web, measuring 1.2m by 17.5cm
* 100% cotton thread (I used a dark blue, green and purple) for sewing round the circles and stitching on the binding
* 18in x 18in (45.7cm x 45.7cm) inner cushion
* Iron
* Fabric scissors
* Ruler
* Pencil
* Compass
* Pins
* Quilter's safety pins
* Sewing machine with walking foot
* Needle

•• Ready

* Iron all your pieces of fabric.
* Cut out four binding strips, one from each fat quarter. Each should measure 3¼in x 19in (8.2cm x 48.2cm).
* To make your circle templates, use a compass to draw three circles measuring 5in (12.7cm), 3in (7.6cm) and 2in (5.1cm) in diameter. Cut the templates out of card or template plastic.
* Prepare the fusible web by cutting out squares as follows: three 5½in (14cm) squares for the 5in (12.7cm) circles, six 3½in (8.9cm) squares for the 3in (7.6cm) circles, and five 2½in (6.3cm) squares for the 2in (5.1cm) circles.
* Iron the fusible web squares on to the back of the fat quarters as follows: on the pink check fabric, iron one large, one medium and two small squares; on the blue flowered fabric, iron one large, one medium and one small square; on the blue spotted fabric, iron two medium and one small square; and on the green fabric, iron one large, two medium and one small square.
* Using your templates, draw a circle on to the paper backing of the fusible web and cut them out.

••• Sew

1 Remove the paper backing from the back of the circles and place the circles on the cushion front. Take time to play around with placement; you can either copy this layout or choose your own. The circles can go in any order, as long as you leave a 1in (2.5cm) border round the edge of each one.

2 When you are happy with how the cushion front looks, pin the circles in place. Then iron each circle to secure, removing the pins as you go.

3 Lay down the backing material, place the wadding (batting) on top, then place your cushion front on top in the centre, with the right side up. Smooth the layers so they are flat, then pin together using quilter's safety pins; pin every 4in (10.2cm), working from the centre out. Baste the layers to secure.

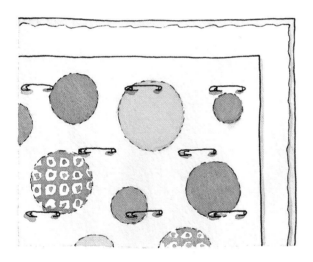

4 Prepare the sewing machine to stitch each circle around its edge. Put the walking foot on the sewing machine and set the machine to a zigzag stitch width 3.5, length 2. Place the cushion front under the foot. Line up the edge of the first circle you are going to sew (the centre circle) under the needle. Hold on to the thread from the needle and lower then raise the needle. When the needle is raised, pull on the thread and this will bring the bobbin thread through.

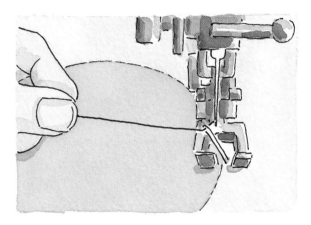

5 Hold the threads to the back and start sewing round the circle. Take your time, and stop every so often to re-adjust the position of the fabric if needed. The trick to getting the stitch looking neat is to keep the majority of the zigzag on the circle. When you get to the stitch where you started, carry on sewing two or three stitches, so they overlap. Take your sewing from the machine, making sure you leave long ends.

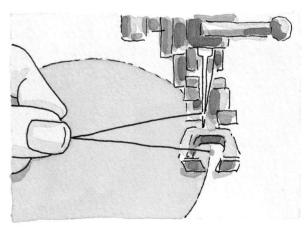

6 Using the wrong end of a needle, unpick a few stitches where the zigzag overlaps, so it ends up looking like it is a piece of continuous stitching, and where you started and finished the sewing is invisible. Thread a needle with the threads and sew them through to the back of the fabric. Tie the threads in a reef knot, and trim. These ends will not be seen as they are inside the cushion. Sew all the circles in the same way. Sew the circles in the middle first, working your way out to the ones near the edge.

< 6 >

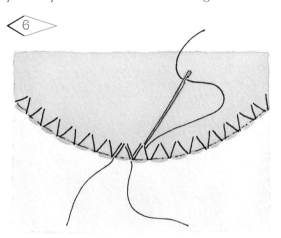

7 Trim the wadding (batting) and backing level with the front of the cushion.

8 Prepare the backing pieces. On one long edge of each, iron a ½in (1.3cm) hem, then fold it over again and iron a 1in (2.5cm) hem. Stitch this down using a straight stitch and toning thread.

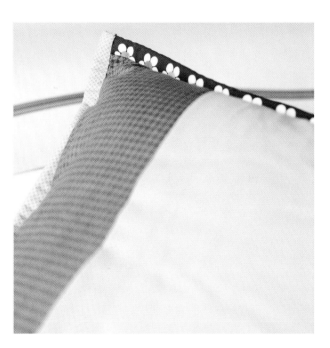

9 Layer the cushion. Place the front down on a flat surface, right side down, then place the two backing pieces on top, right side up. Make sure they are lined up square on the front, then pin all the way round. Turn the cushion over so the front is facing you and pin from the front. When secure, remove the pins from the back of the cushion.

10 To prepare the binding, iron the four strips in half widthways. Pin the binding on two opposite sides of the cushion front. Sew in place using a ½in (1.3cm) seam allowance. Take the binding round to the back and slipstitch to hold it in place, making sure to sew only through the fabric and wadding (batting), not to the other side. Trim the ends so they are level with the sides of the cushion.

9

10

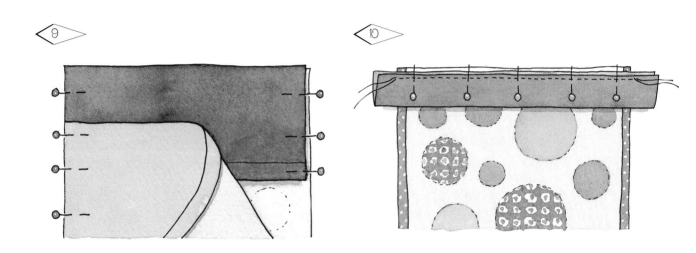

11 Repeat with the other two sides of the cushion, making sure you leave 1in (2.5cm) extra fabric at each side to fold in the ends to make tidy corners.

12 Carefully fill the cover with your inner cushion.

Take it further...
Try the same technique with
different-shaped cushions, such
as hearts, stars or ovals.

Twirling Windmills Quilt

This quilt is made from a traditional design that uses one shape, the half-square triangle, which is then repeated to give a spinning, windmill-type pattern. If you are a beginner, these triangles may look complex but they are really very straightforward to make. The quilt top uses just two fabrics, which is a dream when it comes to choosing colours or patterns for a project! To make it work you need contrast, either a light and a dark fabric, or two different colours. The squares are quite big so don't be afraid ofusing a larger scale pattern. This quilt has been quilted in straight lines, which is a good technique to try if you are new to machine quilting, as the binding hides where you start and finish.

FINISHED SIZE: 42¼in x 57½in (107.3cm x 146cm)

•Get

* 44in x 44in (110cm x 110cm) light fabric
* 44in x 44in (110cm x 110cm) dark fabric
* 51in x 65in (130cm x 165cm) backing fabric
* 51in x 65in (130cm x 165cm) wadding (batting)
* 16in x 44in (40cm x 110cm) binding fabric
* Thread for piecing
* Machine quilting thread
* Thread for binding
* Rotary cutter, acrylic ruler and self-healing mat
* Scissors
* Iron
* Ruler and pencil
* Chalk marker (optional)
* Sewing machine, ¼in (0.6cm) foot and walking foot
* Pins
* Quilter's safety pins
* Sharps sewing needle

••Ready

* Cut your fabrics using a rotary cutter. You need to cut 24 squares measuring 8in (20.3cm) from each of the two fabrics. Make a pile of light and a pile of dark squares, with the direction of the print facing the same way.

••• Sew

1 Take one of the light-coloured fabric squares and place it right side down. Using a pencil or chalk marker and ruler, draw a line from the top left corner to the bottom right corner.

2 Place the light square on top of a dark square, right sides together, and sew a line ¼in (0.6cm) away from the drawn line. Turn the square around and sew another line ¼in (0.6cm) away from the pencil line on the opposite side.

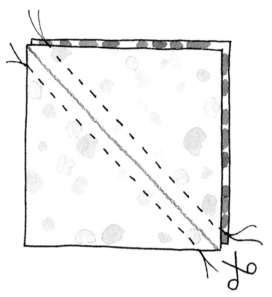

3 Cut down the central drawn line, using a rotary cutter or scissors. You now have two units. Press, with the seams together, towards the darker fabric. You now have two half-square triangles.

◁ 3 ▷

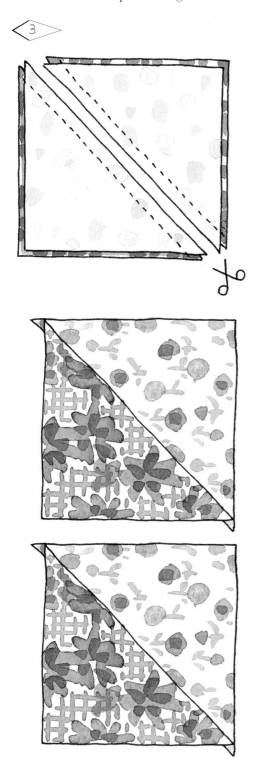

4 Lay four of the half-square triangles out on a table. Spin each square around until you end up with the design shown below. Sew the top two together, then the bottom two together, and press the seams alternate ways. Lay them together, right sides facing, and insert a pin where the central seams meet.

◁ 4 ▷

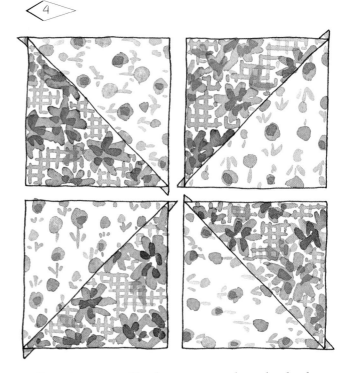

Sew, then press. You have now made a pinwheel unit. Carry on making these with the rest of your squares; you need to end up with 12.

5 Lay out the squares, all facing in the same direction. Lay out a design three squares across, and four squares down. Sew together in rows, then stitch the rows together.

Repeat steps 1 to 3 with the remaining fabric.

6 Assemble the quilt. Lay the backing fabric out, right side down, and smooth. Use masking tape to secure the backing to a flat surface, such as a table or floor, which will help keep it flat while you assemble the layers. Make sure it is not pulled too tight. Lay the wadding (batting) on top and smooth. Place the quilt top on the wadding (batting) and backing, ensuring it is positioned in the middle. Smooth again, then use quilter's safety pins to hold the layers together. Starting in the centre, pin every 4–6in (10.2–15.2cm) in rows, to make a grid format.

7 This quilt has been machine quilted in straight lines across the surface. Line the edge of the walking foot against the line of each row to quilt straight lines. Position the quilt under the foot of your sewing machine at the starting point. Hold on to the thread from the needle and lower then raise the needle. When the needle is up, pull on the thread and this will bring the bobbin thread through. Hold the threads to the back and sew about four or five stitches on your machine's shortest setting to secure the thread. Stop, change the stitch length to 3 and start quilting across. Remove any quilter's pins that get in the way of stitching while you are quilting. When you get to the end of the row, stop with the needle down. Set the stitch length back to its shortest setting and make four or five stitches to secure. Take the quilt out from the machine and trim the threads.

Alternate which side you start from on each row so it does not pull the quilt out of shape.

 7

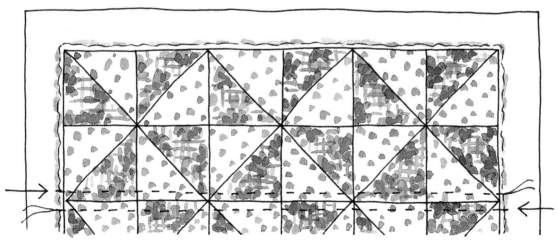

8 To make the binding, cut six strips measuring 2¼in (5.7cm) wide from your binding fabric. Join them together on a 45-degree angle, press the seam open and cut down the seam allowance if necessary. Fold the binding in half, wrong side together, and press, then tuck in a ½in (1.3cm) hem at one end of the binding and press.

9 Trim the wadding (batting) and backing so they are level with the quilt top.

10 Starting on one side of the quilt, pin the binding to the front with the raw edges together. Start one-third of the way down on one side, leaving a tail of binding 2½in (6.3cm) long, from the end which has had the raw edge turned in. Using a walking foot on your sewing machine, sew the binding to the quilt front, taking a ¼in (0.6cm) seam allowance. It helps to pin the binding in place as you sew each side, removing the pins as they get to the edge of the walking foot. When you get to ¼in (0.6cm) before the edge, backstitch to secure. (If you need to, place a pin in the quilt to mark this point.) Take the quilt from the machine, then fold the binding up away from the quilt top, then fold back down. Pin to secure. Start sewing from the corner, taking a ¼in (0.6cm) seam allowance. Repeat at the other three corners.

When you get to 4in (10.2cm) before your starting point, stop sewing. To finish the binding, tuck the end of the binding in the folded end. Trim the excess binding 1in (2.5cm) beyond the hem so it overlaps. Pin and finish sewing.

11 Turn the quilt over, fold the binding to the back and slipstitch, covering the line of machine sewing. At the corners, fold the mitre in on the back so it looks the same as the front and secure with a couple of stitches.

Take it further...
Reduce the size of the squares you start with to make a quick cot quilt.

Tips

When sewing half-square triangles, play around with their layout before sewing them together. This simple shape can make a variety of patterns in patchwork, including diamonds, hourglass and chevrons.

If you are making pinwheels for a quilt and want them to finish a specific size, cut your squares with an additional 7/8in (2.2cm) on to the finished size you want.

Scooter Strips Wall Hanging

This wall hanging is a quirky take on the traditional log cabin quilt block. It uses fabric of different widths to make the central block off-centre. Adding border strips to the bottom and left-hand side accentuates the wonkiness even more.

You can have great fun choosing the fabric for the central block. I used a scooter motif as this quilt was made for a boy's bedroom, but you could use a sewing theme print for a wall hanging in a sewing room, or a computer print for an office. Try to choose a print that uses different colours, and then match your other fabrics to these colours.

FINISHED SIZE: 24in x 25.75in (60.96cm x 65.41cm)

• Get

* 10in (25cm) border fabric
* 4½in x 5½in (11.4cm x 14cm) fabric for centre
* 5 fat quarters
* Thread for piecing
* 32in x 36in (80 x 90cm) backing fabric
* 32in x 36in (80 x 90cm) wadding (batting)
* Machine quilting thread
* 8in (20cm) binding fabric
* Thread for binding
* Rotary cutter, acrylic ruler and self-healing mat (optional)
* Small sticky labels
* Sewing machine, 5¼in (0.6cm) foot and walking foot
* Scissors
* Iron
* Quilter's safety pins
* Fabric pen
* Pins
* Sharps sewing needle

• • Ready

* From the border fabric, cut the following strips across the width: one strip, 2½in (6.3cm) wide; and four strips, 1½in (3.8cm) wide. Put to one side.
* Cut the centre fabric into a rectangle measuring 5½in x 4½in (14cm x 11.4cm).
* From each of the five fat quarters cut a 2in x 4½in (5cm x 11.4cm) wide strip across the width. Then cut this into: three strips measuring 1in x 4½in (2.5cm x 11.4cm); two strips measuring 1½in x 4½in (3.8cm x 11.4cm); two strips measuring 2in x 4½in (5cm x 11.4cm); and two strips measuring 2½in x 4½in (6.3cm x 11.4cm). Put to one side for making the strip border later.
* Cut from each fat quarter, across the width, a strip measuring 1in (2.5cm) wide; a strip measuring 1½in (3.8cm) wide; a strip measuring 2in (5cm) wide; and a strip measuring 2½in (6.3cm) wide.

Ready continued on page 74.

·· Ready

* In this pattern, each fabric has a letter to correspond with the sewing order:
* Fabric A (red squiggle)
* Fabric B (red and blue circles)
* Fabric C (brown check)
* Fabric D (blue dot)
* Fabric E (cream)
* Choose which order you wish to sew your fabrics then stick a note on to each strip saying what letter the fabric corresponds to, and the width. This saves time and confusion when piecing.

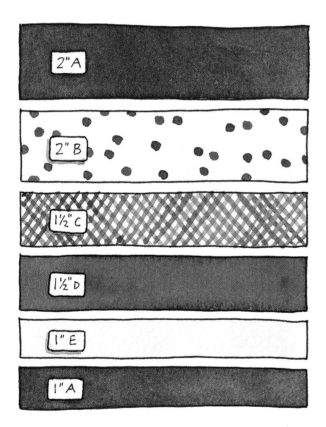

··· Sew

1 All seams are sewn using a ¼in (0.6cm) seam. Take the centre piece of fabric, and the 2in (5cm) wide strip in fabric A. Place the strip level with the bottom of the rectangle, right sides together. Sew, then trim the ends of the strip level with the sides of the rectangle. Press, with the seams together and facing outwards from the centre piece of fabric.

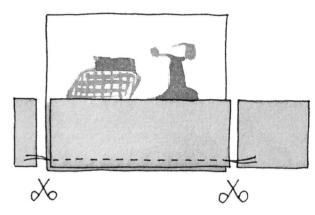

2 Take the 2in (5cm) wide strip in fabric B. Place right sides together on the left-hand side of the centre fabric. Sew as before, then trim the ends level with the fabric. Press, with the seams facing outwards from the centre piece of fabric.

3 Take the 1in (2.5cm) wide strip in fabric C. Line it up with the edge of the top of the centre piece, right sides together. Sew together, then trim the ends level with the fabric. Press, with the seams facing away from the centre piece of fabric.

3

4 Take the 1in (2.5cm) wide strip in fabric D. Place it level with the edge of the right-hand side of the centre fabric, right sides together. As before, sew, then trim the ends level with the fabric. Press, with the seam facing outwards from the centre fabric.

5 Keep sewing strips on in the same way, adding a strip to each side in a clockwise order, trimming them, then pressing, and then adding the next strip. Attach them in the following order:

Bottom fabric E 2½in (6.3cm) strip
Left fabric A 2½in (6.3cm) strip
Top fabric E 1½in (3.8cm) strip
Right fabric B 1½in (3.8cm) strip
Bottom fabric D 2in (5cm) strip
Left fabric C 2in (5cm) strip
Top fabric A 1in (2.5cm) strip
Right fabric E 1in (2.5cm) strip
Bottom fabric B 2½in (6.3cm) strip
Left fabric D 2½in (6.3cm) strip
Top fabric B 1in (2.5cm) strip
Right fabric A 1½in (3.8cm) strip
Bottom fabric C 2½in (6.3cm) strip
Left fabric E 2in (5cm) strip
Top fabric C 1½in (3.8cm) strip
Right fabric D 1½in (3.8cm) strip

6 Take one of the 2½in (6.3cm) wide border strips. Measure the width of your patchwork across the middle and cut a strip to this size. Sew to the bottom of the patchwork piece and press.

7 Make the strippy border for the bottom of the wall hanging. Take the 4½in (11.4cm) wide strips and lay them out, making sure the colours and widths look positioned in a random way. You can also cut down any of the strips left from the log cabin to 4½in (11.4cm) wide to use them up. When you are happy with how the strip looks, join the pieces together. If it ends up slightly too long, trim the ends. Press, then sew the strip on to the bottom of the wall hanging. Press again.

7

8 Take the rest of the 2½in (6.3cm) wide border strip. Measure the length of the piece of patchwork and cut a strip to this size. Sew it on to the left-hand side of the wall hanging and press.

9 Make the strippy border for the side of the wall hanging. Take the 4½in (11.4cm) strips and lay them out, making sure the colours and widths look random. When you are happy with how they look, join them together. If the border ends up slightly too long, trim to size. Press, then sew the strip on to the left-hand side of the wall hanging. Press again.

10 Border the wall hanging. Measure the length, then take two of the 2in (5cm) wide border strips and cut them to this size. Sew one on to each side of the wall hanging and press. Measure the width of the hanging, then cut the two other 2in (5cm) wide border strips to this size. Sew on to the top and bottom of the wall hanging and press.

11 Assemble your quilt. Lay out the backing fabric right side down. Smooth it out until it is flat. Lay the wadding (batting) on top and smooth it so it is flat. Place the quilt top on the wadding (batting) and backing, ensuring it is positioned in the middle. Smooth again, so all three layers are flat. Use quilter's safety pins to hold the layers together. Starting in the centre, insert a pin every 4–6in (10.2–15.2cm) in rows, in a grid format.

12 The log cabin centre has been machine quilted in a spiral. You can either follow the fabric using the edge of the foot on your sewing machine or mark the quilting line on first. Use a ruler and a fabric marker to draw the line.

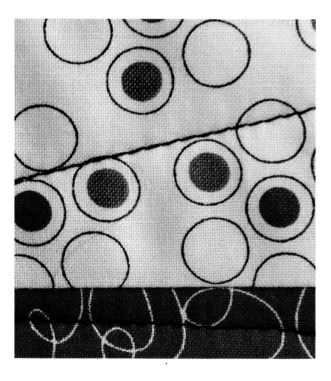

Place the walking foot on the sewing machine and set it up with machine quilting thread. Work from the middle of the spiral outwards. Bring the bobbin thread up to the front. Take four or five stitches on the shortest stitch setting, then re-set the stitch length to 3. Sew following the marked line. When you get to a corner, keep the needle down through the fabric, but lift up the presser foot. Carefully turn the quilt around until it is positioned ready to sew the next line.

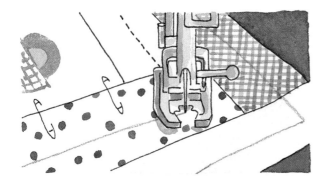

Start sewing again and repeat the process every time you want to change direction. When you get to the end of the quilting, stop ½in (1.3cm) before the end and reduce the stitch length as before. Make four or five stitches, then take the quilt from the sewing machine and snip the thread.

13 The two strip borders have been quilted in a zigzag, with the direction of each line going at different angles. Draw the quilting line on the border and sew as before.

◁ 13 ▷

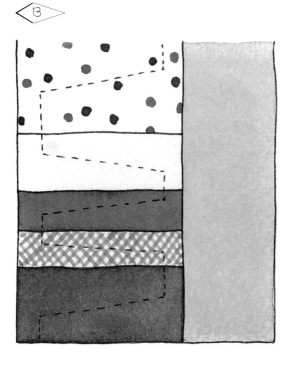

Take it further

Personalize the wall hanging by embroidering a picture or lettering in the central square.

14 Trim the backing and wadding (batting) level with the quilt top. Cut three strips 2½in (6.3cm) wide from the binding fabric and join the strips together at a 45-degree angle. Press the seams open. Fold the binding in half, wrong side together, and press. Fold under a ½in (1.3cm) hem at one end of the binding and press. Start one-third of the way down on one side, leaving a tail of binding 2½in (6.3cm) long, from the end which has had the raw edge turned in. Using a walking foot on your sewing machine, sew the binding to the quilt front, using a ³⁄₈in (0.9cm) seam allowance. It helps to pin the binding in place as you sew each side, removing the pins as they get to the edge of the walking foot. When you get to the end of the side, stop sewing ³⁄₈in (0.9cm) before the edge, and backstitch to secure. (If you need to, place a pin in the quilt to mark this point.) Take the quilt from the machine, then fold the binding up away from the quilt top, then fold back down to create a neat corner. Pin. Start sewing from the corner, with a ³⁄₈in (0.9cm) seam allowance again. Repeat at the other three corners.

When you get to 4in (10.2cm) before your starting point, stop sewing. To finish the binding, tuck the end of the binding in the folded end. Trim the excess binding 1in (2.5cm) beyond the hem so it overlaps. Pin and finish sewing.

15 Turn the quilt over, fold the binding to the back and slipstitch, covering the line of machine sewing. At the corners, fold the mitre in on the back so it looks the same as the front and secure with a couple of stitches.

Here and There Quilt

This stylish quilt combines free-cut patches in blue, grey and yellow-coloured fabric to create a lovely contemporary effect. The colours would look fresh and neutral in a variety of settings, from a teenager's bedroom to a sitting room wall. If you prefer, you could keep the quilt as a cosy cover when watching late night tv, or even take it on cold winter car journeys to keep out the chill.

The patchwork shapes were easily created by cutting rectangles of fabric into unequal shapes; it is this irregular look that gives the quilt its modern feel.

FINISHED SIZE: 39½in x 46in (100.3cm x 116.8cm)

•Get

* 7 x long quarters (10in x 44in/25cm x 110cm)
* Thread for piecing
* 50in x 55in (130cm x 140cm) fabric for backing
* 50in x 55in (130cm x 140cm) wadding (batting)
* Machine quilting thread
* 16in x 44in (40cm x 110cm) fabric for binding
* Thread for binding (to tone with backing)
* Rotary cutter, acrylic ruler and self-healing mat
* Pins
* Sewing machine, ¼in (0.6cm) foot and walking foot
* Iron
* Scissors
* Water-soluble pen (or marking tool for quilting)
* Long ruler
* Low-tack masking tape
* Quilter's safety pins
* Kitchen paper
* Sharps sewing needle

••Ready

* From each long quarter, use a rotary cutter, acrylic ruler and cutting mat to cut six rectangles, each measuring 8in x 7in (20.3cm x 17.8cm). Lay the fabrics out into 14 piles, each containing three different fabrics.

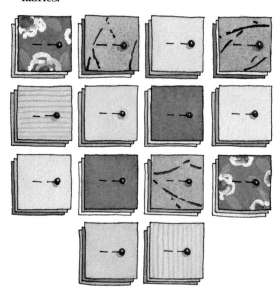

• • • Sew

1 Lay one of the piles on a cutting mat, right sides up, ensuring the edges are level with each other. Using a rotary cutter and ruler, cut the pile into three pieces, changing the angle with each cut. Cut across the length of the fabric (the 8in/20.3cm side), and make sure you don't cut within 1in (2.5cm) of the edge of the fabric, as this can get lost in the seam allowance when you sew it back together.

◁ 1 ▷

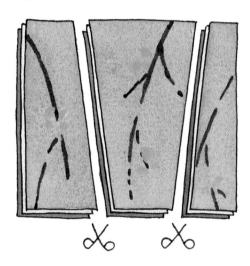

2 Keeping the fabric pile in the position it is in on the board, separate the three fabrics from the left-hand side. Place a different centre fabric next to them, then finally place a different fabric on the right-hand side.

◁ 2 ▷

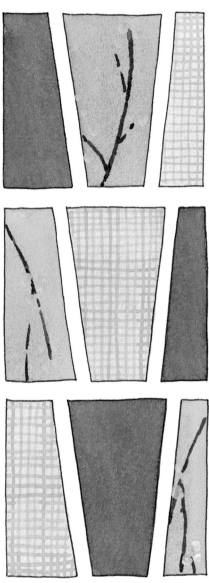

3 In the order the fabrics are laid out, pin then sew them together to make three patchwork pieces. Allow a ¼in (0.6cm) seam allowance.

4 Repeat the above steps with the remaining piles of fabric. When they are all sewn, press each piece with the seams to one side.

5 Lay the fabric out, six pieces across and seven down. Alternate the direction of each piece, so the first piece has vertical seams, the next horizontal and so on. Once they are laid out, check that the prints and colours are evenly distributed. Swap the pieces around if necessary.

When laying out the pieces, play around with the arrangement. My quilt alternates the direction the fabric faces, but you can also get an interesting effect from a quilt where you have all the pieces facing in the same direction. However you decide to lay them out, the squares are sewn together in the same way.

6 When you are happy with the layout, start piecing the units together. Sew the pieces into rows, allowing a ¼in (0.6cm) seam allowance.

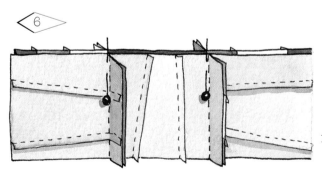

7 Sew the rows together. Take the top row and place it on an ironing board, right side down. Press the seams together with them facing the same way. Then turn the row over and give it another press from the front. Iron the second row in the same way, this time pressing the seams together in the opposite direction.

8 Place the two rows on top of each other with right sides together. Line up the squares and you will see that where the seams have been pressed in different directions they lock in. Pinch the seam allowances to make sure the seams are nestled in, then place a pin through the fabric to hold them in place.

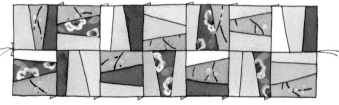

Repeat this at each seam along the row. Sew along this row, taking the pins out as they go under the foot so you don't stitch over them. Join the rest of the rows in the same way, taking care to press the seams on each row in alternate directions.

9 Press the quilt top and snip off any loose threads. Mark the quilting lines on top of the patchwork using a water-soluble pen and a ruler. It helps if you have a long ruler, such as an acrylic patchwork ruler or metre stick. I quilted a long, slightly diagonal line from the top of the row on one side to the bottom of the row on the other. By starting on the row where I last ended, it creates a zigzag movement across the quilt.

9

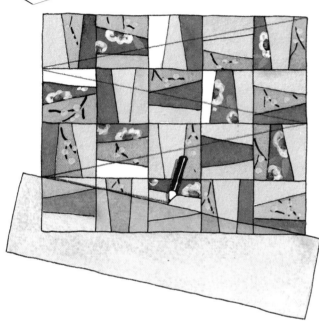

10 To assemble the quilt, first press the backing fabric, then lay it right side down and smooth it flat. Use masking tape to secure the backing to a flat surface; this helps keep it flat while you assemble the quilt. Make sure it is not pulled too tight. Lay the wadding (batting) on top. Smooth down, then place the quilt top on the wadding (batting) and backing, positioning it in the middle. Smooth again, so all three layers are flat. Use quilter's safety pins to hold the layers together. Starting in the centre, pin every 4–6in (10.2–15.2cm) in rows, to make a grid format.

11 Set up the sewing machine with a walking foot and machine quilting thread, and set the stitch length to your machine's shortest setting. Position the quilt under the foot of your sewing machine at the starting point. Hold on to the thread from the needle and lower then raise the needle. When the needle is up, pull on the thread and this will bring the bobbin thread through. Hold the threads to the back of your work and sew about four or five stitches to secure the thread. Stop, change the stitch length to 3, then start quilting your design. Machine quilt following the straight lines drawn with the water-soluble pen. Remove any quilter's pins that get in the way of stitching while you are quilting. When you get to the end of your stitching, stop with the needle down. Set the stitch length back to its shortest setting and make four or five stitches to secure. Take the quilt out from the machine and trim the threads. Remove the water-soluble marks by gently dabbing with a piece of damp kitchen paper.

12 When the quilting is complete, cut the wadding (batting) and backing level with the edge of the quilt top, and remove any remaining quilter's pins.

13 To make approximately 5¼yd (4.8m) of binding, cut strips 2½in (6.3cm) wide from the binding fabric. Draw a 45-degree line on the wrong side of one of the strips. Line it up with another strip, wrong sides together, and stitch along the line, trim the seam allowance to ¼in (0.6cm) and press the seams open. Repeat to join all the strips. Fold the binding in half, wrong side together, and press. Then fold under a ½in (1.3cm) hem at one end of the binding and press.

14 Pin the binding to the front of the quilt, with the raw edge of the binding level with the raw edge of the quilt. Start one-third of the way down on one side of the quilt, leaving a tail of binding 2½in (6.3cm) long, from the end which has had the raw edge turned in. Using a walking foot on your sewing machine, sew the binding to the quilt front, taking a ³⁄₈in (0.9cm) seam allowance. It helps to pin the binding in place as you sew each side, removing the pins as they get to the edge of the walking foot. When you get to the end of the side, stop sewing ³⁄₈in (0.9cm) before the edge, and backstitch to secure. (If you need to, place a pin in the quilt to mark this point.) Take the quilt from the machine, fold the binding up away from the quilt top and then fold it back down. Pin to secure. Start sewing from the corner, with a ³⁄₈in (0.9cm) seam allowance. Repeat at the other three corners.

◁ 14 ▷

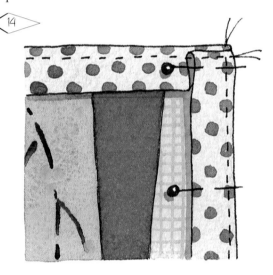

When you get to 4in (10.2cm) before your starting point, stop sewing. To finish the binding, tuck the end of the binding in the folded end. Trim the excess binding 1in (2.5cm) beyond the hem so it overlaps. Pin and finish sewing.

15 Turn the quilt over, fold the binding to the back and slipstitch using a Sharps sewing needle, covering the line of machine sewing. At the corners, fold the mitre in on the back so it looks the same as the front and secure with a couple of stitches.

Take it further

Use the same technique, but rather than cutting the fabric into three pieces, cut it into four, or even nine.

Box du Jour

The traditional technique of broderie perse has inspired this box. The name is given to a technique where motifs are cut from one fabric, then sewn on to another piece. It was widely used from the late 18th to the early 19th century, when chintz fabric was expensive and so highly prized. My modern take on the technique uses fusible web to attach the motif to a backing fabric, then the edge is sewn down using blanket stitch. Most sewing machines have this stitch, but if yours doesn't, it is easy to hand-sew a blanket stitch around the edge of the motif. I have styled my box for a kitchen, where it can be used as a handy container for fruit, vouchers or paper and pens. You can use the box in any room you choose – just adapt the motifs as you wish.

FINISHED SIZE: 5¼in (13.3cm) square

Get

* 18in (45.7cm) square of card for template
* Fat quarter fabric for front
* Fat quarter fabric for lining
* Selection of fabric with motifs
* Fusible web (size depends on how many motifs you wish to appliqué)
* Fat quarter calico for backing (this will not be visible)
* Fat quarter wadding (batting)
* Thread for assembling box
* Thread for stitching around appliqué
* 2¼in x 44in (5.7cm x 110cm) fabric for binding
* Thread for binding (to tone with binding fabric)
* 8 buttons for sides (optional)
* Scissors
* Iron
* Ruler
* Disappearing fabric pen or chalk marker
* Quilter's safety pins
* Sewing machine, ¼in (0.6cm) foot, walking foot and clear zigzag foot
* Sharps sewing needle
* Pins
* Rotary cutter, acrylic ruler and self-healing mat (optional)

Ready

* To prepare the templates, cut an 18in (45.7cm) square out of card and then a 5¾in (1.9cm) square of card. Place the smaller square level with the corner of the larger square and draw round it. Repeat on every corner. Cut out the small square shapes with scissors, and you will end up with a piece of card that looks like this.

Ready continued on page 74.

·· Ready

❊ Draw around the template on to the back of the fabric for the box front and on the lining fabric. Use scissors to cut out the fabric, following the line. Put the lining to one side.

❊ Choose your appliqué motifs and cut them from the fabric, adding ½in (1.3cm) extra around the edge. Cut a piece of fusible web slightly smaller than the piece to be applied. Place on to the back on the motif with the adhesive side down and press with an iron to fix. Trim the motif, either leaving a small border all the way around or cut right on the edge of the shape, depending on how you want it to look.

❊ When you have cut all the motifs, peel the paper backing off the fusible web. Lay the motifs down on the right side of the box fabric. Remember, when deciding how to lay out the motifs, the square in the middle of the fabric is the base of the box. Also be careful not to put them too near any of the edges as they will be lost in the seam allowance. When they are positioned correctly, press with an iron to fix into place. Use a ruler and disappearing fabric pen or chalk marker to draw around the centre square.

❊ Press and lay the calico on a table. Place the wadding (batting) on top and smooth down. Lay the box front on top in the centre, right side up; smooth the layers, then secure with quilter's safety pins.

··· Sew

1 Sew along the drawn lines to make a square in the centre of the box. This helps to square up the base for later.

2 Set up the sewing machine for blanket stitch. Use your machine manual for guidance, and test the stitch on scrap fabric to make sure you are happy with the width and length. To stitch around a motif, place the fabric under the presser foot, hold the thread, then lower the needle down through the fabric at your starting point. Raise the needle, then pull on the thread. This will bring the bobbin thread to the front. Put the threads to the back and start sewing around the motif. Stop sewing when you get back to where you started and take the fabric from the sewing machine, leaving a thread at least 6in (15.2cm) long. Repeat to stitch around each motif. Use a Sharps sewing needle to take the loose threads through to the back, knot them to secure, and trim to leave a 1in (2.5cm) tail.

If you are hand sewing instead of using a sewing machine, use blanket stitch to sew around the edge of each shape.

3 Trim the wadding (batting) and backing level with the box front.

⟨ 3 ⟩

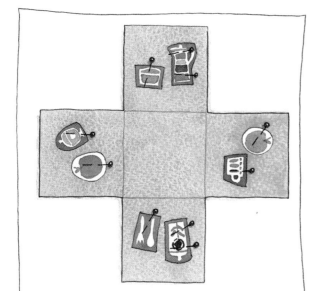

4 To sew the sides of the box, use a walking foot on your sewing machine, as there are lots of layers, and leave a ¼in (0.6cm) seam allowance. Fold the box in half, right sides together. Pin the side to be sewn. Starting at the bottom of the box, sew a few stitches, then reverse to secure. Carry on sewing up to the top of the seam. Repeat on the opposite seam.

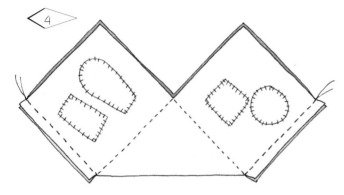

Open up the box and sew the third seam in the same way. Open up the box again, then fold to sew the remaining seam. Turn the box out, so the right side is facing outwards, and use your fingers to ease it gently into shape.

5 To sew the lining, leave a ¼in (0.6cm) seam allowance, and sew the sides as before to make a box shape. Once sewn, place the lining inside the box, with the right side facing outwards.

6 Position the seams of the lining with the seams of the box and pin together. Secure the lining to the box by sewing around the top of the box as close to the edge as possible.

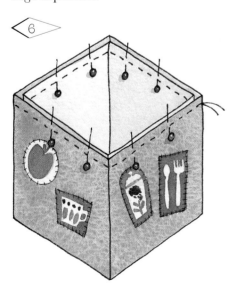

Take it further
Adapt the size of the pattern to make larger or smaller boxes.

7 To make the binding, take the strip of binding fabric and iron it in half widthways, with the wrong side together. Fold in a ½in (1.3cm) hem at one end and press.

8 Place the binding on the outside of the box. Line up the raw edge of the binding with the raw edge of the box and pin. Using a walking foot, start 3in (7.6cm) away from the end with the hem and sew leaving a ⅜in (0.9cm) seam allowance. When you get near to where you started, tuck the end of the binding in the hem and pin. Continue sewing until you get to the place where you started.

9 Fold the binding over inside the box, and slipstitch down using a toning thread.

10 I have added buttons to the top of my box to give it a square shape, but these are optional. If you wish to add buttons, pinch a side seam, then sew a button on each side at the same time, pulling the thread tight to pull the side of the box in. Repeat on all four sides.

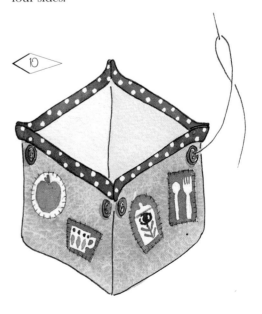

Grab and Sew Quilt

This quilt is all about convenience. One printed and one plain Jelly Roll are all you need for the quilt top, which cuts down the time spent in preparing the fabric. In case you are new to Jelly Rolls, they are pre-cut rolls of 40 strips, 2½in (6.3cm) wide and 44in (110cm) long. The strips in this quilt are cut and sewn in batches so it makes this an ideal project if you can only dedicate short bursts of time to sewing. I have been known to sneak in a quick 15 minutes at the sewing machine with projects like this before the school run!

FINISHED SIZE: 49½in x 79½in (125.7cm x 201.9cm)

• Get

* 1 printed Jelly Roll
* 1 plain Jelly Roll
* Thread for piecing
* 90in x 60in (220cm x 150cm) backing (look for extra wide backing fabric or join fabric together)
* 90in x 60in (220cm x 150cm) wadding (batting)
* Thread for binding
* Pins
* Rotary cutter, acrylic ruler and self-healing mat
* Sewing machine and walking foot
* Iron
* Sharps sewing needle
* Scissors
* Supplies to assemble and quilt (if you are quilting this project yourself and not using a long arm quilter)

•• Ready

* The quilt is made in sets of three. Lay the Jelly Roll strips out and select two printed fabrics and one plain; pin together. Try to ensure that the printed fabric in the set has different colours and patterns. Repeat with all the strips until you have 20 sets.

••• *Sew*

1 Take one set of three strips. Using a rotary cutter, mat and ruler, trim the selvedge off the end, then from each strip cut: two squares measuring 2½in (6.3cm), three strips measuring 4in (10.2cm) long, and two strips measuring 8in (20.3cm) long.

Cut one of the 2½in (6.3cm) squares from each strip in half, so you have two pieces that measure 2½in x 1¼in (6.3cm x 3.2cm).

Cut one of the 4in (10.2cm) strips from each strip in half so you have two pieces measuring 4in x 1¼in (10.2cm x 3.2cm)

2 Lay out the fabrics with a 2½in (6.3cm) square in the centre. Then place a 2½in x 1¼in (6.3cm x 3.2cm) strip on the top and bottom. Next add a 4in x 1¼in (10.2cm x 3.2cm) strip on each side, then a 4in x 2½in (10.2cm x 6.3cm) strip on the top and bottom, and finally an 8in x 2½in (20.3cm x 6.3cm) strip on each side. Make three sets, each with a different fabric in the centre, middle and outer edge.

3 Sew the sets together, taking a ¼in (0.6cm) seam allowance. Pick up the centre square and sew on the top and bottom. Press with the seams together, facing out from the centre.

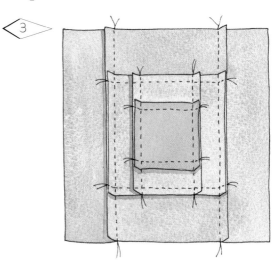

Add the sides and press; keep adding the strips until you have three squares.

4 Once all the sets are sewn, put them into three piles: one pile with a plain centre, one pile with a plain middle, and one pile with a plain outer edge.

Continue this process with each set. Don't be tempted to cut and lay out more than one set at a time, as it is easy to get confused!

Start laying out the rows in this order. The quilt is six squares wide and ten rows long. Once you have laid out a couple of rows, you will notice that the squares with the plain fabric on the outer edges form a diagonal pattern. Move the squares around, always swapping squares that have the plain fabric in the same position. Once you are happy with the layout, check that in each square the strips are going in opposite directions, so one square has the outer strips horizontal, then the next one has them vertical, and so on.

5 Place the first two squares together, right sides facing, and sew leaving a ¼in (0.6cm) seam allowance. Continue adding the squares until the row is joined together. Repeat with the other rows, so the rows are in ten strips.

Place the top row right side down on an ironing board. Press the seams together with them facing the same way. Then turn the row over and give it another press from the front. Iron the second row in the same way, this time pressing the seams together in the opposite direction. Place the two rows on top of each other, right sides together. Line up the squares and you will see that where the seams have been pressed in different directions they lock in. Pinch where the seam allowances meet to make sure that the seams are nestled in, and then insert a pin through the fabric to hold them in place. Repeat at each seam along the row. Leaving a ¼in (0.6cm) seam allowance, stitch along this row, removing the pins as they go under the sewing machine foot, so you don't sew over them.

Use the same technique to join the rest of the rows, taking care to press the seams on each row in alternate directions. When the rows are joined together, press the quilt top.

Tip

Long arm quilters provide a range of services, from assembling your quilt, to quilting and binding it for you, using a frame and a special sewing machine. The service they offer is great if you don't feel confident quilting your work.

6 To make the border for the sides, cut four Jelly Roll strips to 38in (96.5cm). Join two together using a ¼in (0.6cm) seam and press. Then join the other two together and press. Sew the border to the sides of the patchwork, and press open.

Cut two long, plain Jelly Roll strips to measure 40in (101.6cm), then two more short strips to measure 10in (25.4cm). Join the long and short strips together and press. Join the other two strips together and press. Sew to the top and bottom of the quilt. Press the patchwork top.

(Note: if your seam allowance has come out smaller or larger than ¼in (0.6cm), you may need to adjust the size of your border to make it fit. The correct way to measure a quilt is through the middle.)

7 This quilt was sent off to be long arm quilted. I provided the backing fabric and wadding (batting). If you want to do your own quilting, see pages 23–27 for quilting techniques.

8 Use the offcuts from the Jelly Rolls to make a scrap binding. Trim the selvedge off the pieces of the strips that are left, and join the strips together on a 45-degree seam. I joined two printed pieces, then one plain. You need the binding to be approximately 275in (700cm) long. Press the seams open. Fold the binding in half, wrong side together, and press.

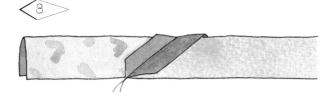

Take it further
Try making the quilt with just three fabrics to create a graphic quilt.

9 Sew the binding on to the quilt. Fold under a 1in (2.5cm) hem at one end of the binding and press. Starting on one side of the quilt, pin the binding to the front with the raw edges together. Start one-third of the way down on one side, leaving a tail of binding 2½in (6.3cm) long, from the end that has had the raw edge turned in. Using a walking foot on your sewing machine, sew the binding to the quilt front, leaving a ³⁄₈in (0.9cm) seam allowance. It helps to pin the binding in place as you sew each side, removing the pins as they get to the edge of the walking foot. When you get to the end of the side, stop sewing ³⁄₈in (0.9cm) before the edge, and backstitch to secure. (If you need to, insert a pin in the quilt to mark this point.) Take the quilt from the machine, then fold the binding up away from the quilt top, then fold it back down and pin. Start sewing from the corner, with a ³⁄₈in (0.9cm) seam allowance. Repeat at the other three corners. When you get to 4in (10.2cm) before your starting point, stop sewing. To finish the binding, tuck the end of the binding in the folded end. Trim the excess binding 1in (2.5cm) beyond the hem so it overlaps. Pin and finish sewing.

10 Turn the quilt over, fold the binding to the back and slipstitch to secure, covering the line of machine sewing. At the corners, fold the mitre in on the back so it looks the same as the front and secure with a couple of stitches.

Summer Sunburst Cushion

Dresden Plate is one of those traditional quilt blocks that never seems to date. This way of making the block combines machine and hand sewing. For this cushion I have made just one block, but it is hard to stop making them, so it may be that you get hooked and make a quilt to go with it.

If you wish to, use just two fabrics for the spokes, but if you have a selection of scraps to use up this would be a good project for them. I made my cushion in pretty pinks and blues, but you could try using muted taupes, or rainbow brights – whatever floats your boat!

FINISHED SIZE: 14in (35.6cm) square

•Get

* 2 pieces of 11in x 15in (27.9cm x 38.1cm) fabric for cushion back
* 6in (15.2cm) square of template plastic
* 20 pieces of 3in x 4½in (7.6cm x 11.4cm) fabric for Dresden spokes
* 6in (15.2cm) square of no-melt template plastic
* Thread for piecing and assembling cushion
* 17in (43.2cm) square of calico for backing for cushion front
* Starch
* 4in (10.2cm) square of fabric for centre circle
* 17in (43.2cm) square of wadding (batting)
* 15in (38.1cm) square of fabric for cushion front
* Perle thread, no 8, for quilting
* Scissors
* Pencil
* Pins
* Sewing machine, ¼in (0.6cm) foot and walking foot
* Knitting needle or bamboo pointer
* Iron
* Sharps sewing needle
* Small paintbrush
* Quilter's safety pins
* Chenille needle

••Ready

* Cut the fabric for the back of the cushion to size and put to one side. Trace the wedge shape (see Templates, page 120) on to a piece of template plastic. Place one of the 3in x 4½in (7.6cm x 11.4cm) pieces of fabric on a table, right side down. Draw around the template on to the wrong side of the fabric then, using scissors, cut out along the line. Repeat with the other 19 pieces.

••• Sew

1 Take one of the wedge-shaped pieces of fabric. Fold it in half, right sides together, and press the fold with your finger. Leaving a ¼in (0.6cm) seam allowance, stitch along the wider end, with the folded edge going through the sewing machine first. Sew ½in (1.3cm), then stop and sew a few stitches in reverse, before continuing to sew along the top. Remove the fabric from the machine. Using scissors, trim the seam allowance at the end you started stitching. This means that you will get a sharper point when you turn the fabric inside out.

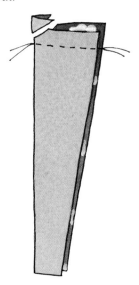

Once the fabric is turned out, use a knitting needle or bamboo pointer to gently push the point out. Press the fabric with the seam facing upwards, ensuring that the seam is in the centre of the fabric.

Repeat this step with the other 19 wedge-shaped pieces of fabric. To speed up the sewing, you can chain stitch them. Lay the fabric out next to the sewing machine, then stitch the first piece. When you get to the end of the fabric, do not cut the thread; instead, lift the presser foot, feed the next piece of fabric under it, and continue sewing. This leaves a few threads in between each piece, which can be cut when they are all sewn.

2 Lay the fabric out until you are happy with the placement. Sew the fabric pieces first into quarters and then into halves.

Take two pieces that are next to each other. Place them right sides together and, leaving a ¼in (0.6cm) seam allowance, start at the pointed end and sew down ½in (1.3cm), stop and take a few reverse stitches. Then continue to sew to the end.

Tip

If you are making lots of Dresden blocks, it is a good idea to buy an acrylic wedge ruler. These are widely available, and using one means that the shapes can be cut quickly using a rotary cutter instead of drawing the shape and cutting out with a pair of scissors.

Press the seams to one side, making sure that all the seams are pressed the same way. This helps the pieces to lie flat. Remember to press from the front as well as from the back.

4 Turn the fabric over. Using scissors, cut the fabric behind the Dresden plate ½in (1.3cm) away from the sewn line, being very careful not to cut through to the front.

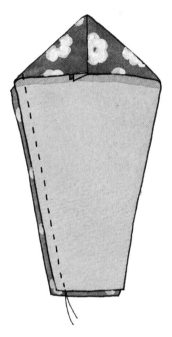

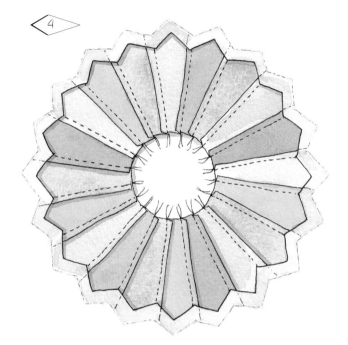

3 Press the backing fabric in half, then open it out and press it in half the other way. Lay the Dresden plate on top, using the crease lines to position the plate in the centre. Pin in place, then slipstitch by hand around the edge to attach to the backing fabric.

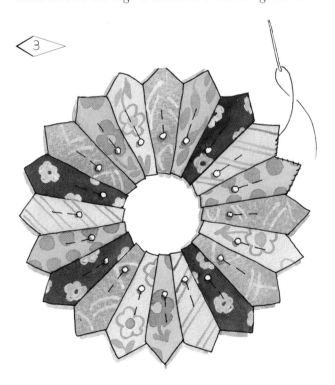

5 To make the circle for the centre, first put some starch in a bowl near the ironing board, and place a small paintbrush next to it. Place the template on the wrong side of the fabric and lightly draw around it using a pencil. Cut out the circle, cutting a generous ¼in (0.6cm) away from the line to give a seam allowance. Thread a Sharps sewing needle and knot the end. Sew a running stitch through the middle of the seam allowance, leaving the thread at the end loose. Place the template in the middle, then pull the ends of the thread to gather the seam allowance in. Hold the threads and press the seam allowance, then use the paintbrush to brush starch all around the seam allowance. Press again. Once the starch is dry, cut the thread and pull out the running stitch. Gently remove the circle template and press again if needed.

6 Position the circle in the middle of the Dresden plate and pin. Slipstitch around the edge.

7 Press the calico and lay it on a table. Place the wadding (batting) on top and smooth. Place the cushion front on top, right side up, making sure it is in the centre. Smooth, then attach the layers by inserting quilter's safety pins through the fabric 4in (10.2cm) apart, in a grid format.

8 Quilt the cushion front using a chenille needle and perle quilting thread. I hand quilted a line just inside the edge of the circle, then another line ¼in (0.6cm) away from the edge of the Dresden. The back will not be seen as it will be inside the cushion so you can start with a knot and finish with a backstitch.

9 Trim the wadding (batting) and backing level with the cushion front.

10 Prepare your backing pieces. On one long edge of each, iron a ½in (1.3cm) hem, then fold it over again and iron a 1in (2.5cm) hem. Sew this down using a straight stitch and toning thread.

11 To layer the cushion, place the front down, right side up, then place the two backing pieces on top, one at each end, right side down. Make sure they are lined up square on the front, then pin all the way around.

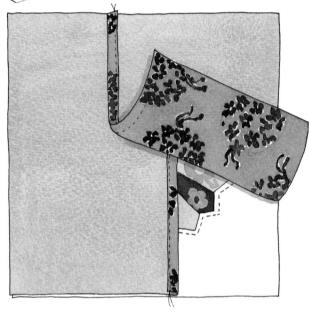

Start two-thirds of the way down one side, then sew all around the edge leaving a ½in (1.3cm) seam allowance. As there are lots of layers, use a walking foot on your sewing machine for this step. Clip the corners, then turn the cushion cover right side out.

Take it further...
Make nine Dresden Plates, sewn on to square backing fabric and join them together to make a small quilt.

Funky Town Wall Hanging

One of my favourite classic patchwork designs is the schoolhouse block, so I decided to make my own version, based on the Victorian terrace houses you see all over Britain. While it may look complex, once you have cut the pieces and laid them out in the correct order, it is quick and easy to sew together. I have hand quilted this wall hanging, but it would also look good machine quilted. As it is small you can have some fun with it!

I came across the black and white window fabric quite by chance and it was fun to use this for the house windows. If you would like a similar look and can't find any suitable fabric, you could try putting some strips of lace up at the windows for curtains.

FINISHED SIZE: 32in x 15¼in (81.3cm x 38.7cm)

• Get

* 12in x 44in (30cm x 110cm) house fabric (use fabric with a non-directional print)
* 10in x 10in (25cm x 25cm) window fabric
* 16in x 4in (40cm x 10cm) door fabric
* 10in x 16in (25cm x 40cm) roof fabric
* 6in x 32in (15cm x 80cm) fat eighth sky fabric
* 6in x 44in (15cm x 110cm) border fabric
* Thread for piecing
* 24in x 35½in (60cm x 90cm) backing fabric
* 24in x 35½in (60cm x 90cm) wadding (batting)
* 3 buttons
* 8in x 44in (20cm x 110cm) binding fabric
* Thread for binding
* Perle thread, no 8, for quilting
* Rotary cutter, acrylic ruler and self-healing mat
* Pins
* Sewing machine and ¼in (0.6cm) foot
* Iron
* Pencil
* Scissors
* Quilter's safety pins
* ¼in (0.6cm) masking tape or other marking tool for quilting
* Sharps sewing needle
* Chenille needle

•• Ready

* As you cut the fabric, it is essential to use the diagram below for reference and to lay the fabric for each house down in the correct order. If you are planning to cut and sew at a later time, make a three photocopies of the template on page 121 and pin the fabric to it to keep it in order.

9½" x 1¼"				
3" x 1¾"	3" x 3"	3" x 2"	3" x 3"	3" x 1¾"
9½" x 2"				
4½" x 2"	3" x 3"	4½" x 2"	4½" x 2½"	4½" x 2"
	3" x 2"			

Ready continued on page 102.

··Ready

* From the house fabric, cut: two strips, 2in (5cm) wide from selvedge to selvedge; one strip, 3in (7.6cm) wide from selvedge to selvedge; and one strip 1¼in (3.2cm) wide from selvedge to selvedge. Cut the 2in (5cm) wide strips into: three pieces 3in (7.6cm) long, nine pieces 4½in (11.4cm) long, and three pieces 9½in (24.1cm) long. Cut the 3in (7.6cm) wide strip into six pieces 1¾in (4.4cm) long, and three pieces 2in (5cm) long. Cut the 1¼in (3.2cm) wide strip into three pieces 9½in (24.1cm) long.

* From the window fabric cut nine 3in (7.6cm) squares. From the door fabric cut a 2½in (6.3cm) wide strip, then cut this into three 4½in (11.4cm) strips.

* From the roof fabric cut three pieces measuring 9½in x 5in (24.1cm x 12.7cm). From the sky fabric cut six 5in (12.7cm) squares. From the border fabric cut two strips measuring 1in x 13½in (2.5cm x 34.3cm), to go between the houses; two strips measuring 1½in x 13½in (3.8cm x 34.3cm) for the sides; and two strips measuring 1½in x 30½in (3.8cm x 77.5cm) for the top and bottom. Put these pieces to one side.

* A ¼in (0.6cm) seam is used at all times when sewing the house together. As this is a small project with lots of pieces, it helps to pin the fabric before sewing, taking the pins out as the fabric goes under the presser foot of the sewing machine.

··· Sew

1 The houses are sewn individually; however, all three have been stitched at the same time to speed up the making process. Start by taking the downstairs window and the piece of the house under it and stitching together. Press to one side, then lay the stitched piece in the correct place on the fabric layout.

◁1▷

2 Sew together the pieces that make up the bottom floor of the house and press. Repeat with the top floor of the house and press. (At this point you will start to see the pieces that make the house come together and the pile of unsewn fabrics looks less scary!)

◁2▷

3 Following the layout, sew the ground floor of the house to the strip above it, and the first floor of the house to the strip that goes above that. Press, then sew the two pieces of the house together.

4 To make the roof, take one of the squares of sky fabric, and draw a diagonal line with a pencil across the back, corner to corner. Place this on the rectangle for the roof, with the three sides level. Sew down the line. Press and trim the seam allowance, open the fabric up and press again. Repeat with the other square on the opposite side of the rectangle.

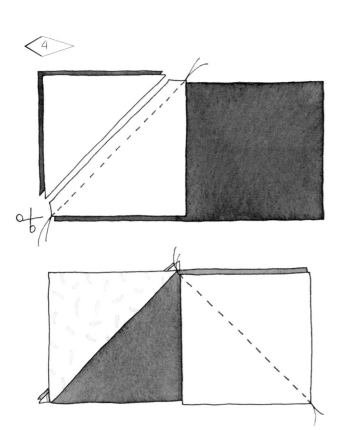

5 With the right sides together, line the roof up with the top of the house and sew together.

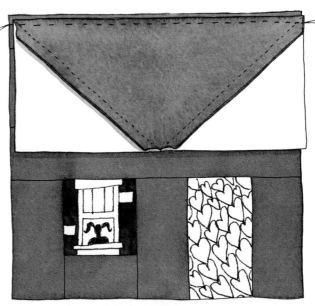

6 Take the narrow border fabric, and sew on to each side of the centre house. Press, then attach the other houses on each side.

7 Sew the side borders on and press; then sew the top and bottom border on. Press and trim any threads.

8 Press the backing fabric, then lay it out, right side down. Lay the wadding (batting) on top and smooth till it is flat. Place the quilt top on the wadding (batting) and backing, ensuring it is positioned in the middle. Use quilter's safety pins to hold the layers together. Starting in the centre, pin every 4–6in (10.2–15.2cm) in rows, to make a grid format.

9 To hand quilt the wall hanging around the edge of the houses, use masking tape or other marking tool to create the guidelines, then stitch along the line using perle quilting thread and a chenille needle. Stitch a button on to each door to make a handle. Have some fun with this stage, adding as much stitching and embellishment as you wish.

10 Cut the wadding (batting) and backing level with the quilt top. Cut three strips from the binding fabric 2½in (6.3cm) wide. Make a length of binding approximately 2¾yd (2.5m) long. Sew the binding to the quilt front, mitring the corners carefully as you go (see page 28).

11 Turn the quilt over and, using toning thread and a Sharps sewing needle, slipstitch the binding down. At the corners, fold the mitre in on the back, so it looks the same as the front.

Take it further
Use graph paper to design your own house, working out all the measurements, including seam allowances.

Spots and Blocks Bookmarks

This small project is the perfect way to dip your toe into the world of free machine quilting. Easy to make in an afternoon, these creative bookmarks use offcuts of fabric so are really inexpensive. As this project makes five bookmarks at a time, keep one for yourself and give the rest as presents.

You can tailor your fabric choices to match the type of books you are making them for, as I have done here, inspired by the iconic, orange Penguin book covers. The spotted black and white fabric provides a graphic contrast, while the satin stitch edging frames each bookmark beautifully.

FINISHED SIZE: 2in x 10in (5cm x 25.4cm)

• Get

* 2 pieces of 9¾in x 7¼in (24.8cm x 18.4cm) fusible web
* 1 piece of 10in x 7½in (25.4cm x 19cm) pelmet Vilene
* 1 piece of 10in x 7½in (25.4cm x 19cm) fabric for back
* 3 pieces of 11in x 4in (27.9cm x 10.2cm) fabric for front
* Thread for machine quilting (I suggest you use standard 100% cotton sewing thread. Once you have some experience in free machine quilting, experiment with other types of thread, such as rayon)
* Thread for edging
* Rotary cutter, acrylic ruler and self-healing mat
* Iron
* Scissors
* Sewing machine, darning foot and zigzag foot
* Pencil and paper

•• Ready

* Take one of the pieces of fusible web. Place it in the centre of the Vilene with the glue (rough) side facing downwards and iron to fix in place. When ironing fusible web, make sure you press the iron down, and do not sweep it from side to side as you can distort it. Peel the paper backing off, then lay the backing fabric on top. Press again, and the backing fabric should now be fixed in place.
* Turn the pelmet Vilene over, place the second piece of fusible web in the centre and press. Leave the paper backing on.

... Sew

1 Using the rotary cutter and ruler, cut lengthways across the fabric for the front in a random way. Alter the angle of the ruler with each cut so that each of the strips looks different.

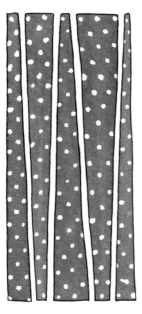

2 Take your piece of Vilene and place it on the ironing board with the backing fabric side facing down. Peel the paper off the fusible web. Lay the fabric strips on top, alternating the fabrics and the angle you place them. Try to lay them so each strip butts up against the next so none of the backing is showing. Once you are happy with how it looks, press till the fusible web holds the strips in place. Trim the edges of the piece so it measures 10in x 7½in (25.4cm x 19cm).

3 Prepare the sewing machine. Check that the bobbin has enough thread, then attach the darning foot and drop or cover the feed dogs. If you are unsure how to drop the feed dogs, check in your sewing machine manual. Set the machine for a standard straight stitch. Draw on a piece of paper the pattern you will be making – I stitched an allover, meandering design across the fabric. With free machine quilting, think of the needle and thread as the pencil drawing the design.

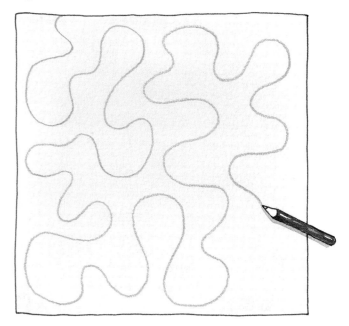

When you are ready to start sewing, begin at the edge of the fabric, and bring the bobbin thread through to the front. Take a couple of stitches in the same spot to secure the thread, then start sewing, moving the piece of fabric to make the pattern. Go at a steady pace; the speed of the machine and how you move the fabric will dictate how large the stitches are and the design you sew. Keep the needle moving across the fabric in a meandering design and when you get to the other end, take a couple of stitches on the spot, then cut the thread. If at this stage you are worrying about your stitching, don't! Once the piece is cut up, it is more flattering to unruly stitches.

4 Cut the piece of fabric into five strips, each one 2in (5cm) wide.

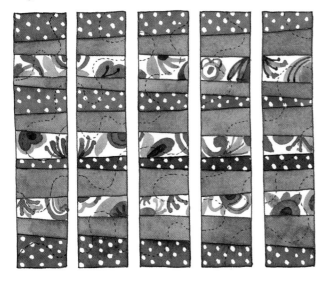

Take it further
Instead of cutting the stitched piece into strips, cut into squares and make coasters. Try out different free-machined designs, practising them on paper first.

5 To edge the bookmarks, set the sewing machine to satin stitch. To do this, put a foot on the sewing machine suitable for zigzag stitch and set the machine length to 0.5, and the width to 3. Raise the feed dogs. Thread the machine with the edging thread. Start sewing two-thirds down one of the long sides and stitch down to the end of the side. When you get to the corner, stop with the needle down, on the edge of the bookmark, lift the foot and pivot the bookmark round. Put the foot down and start stitching again.

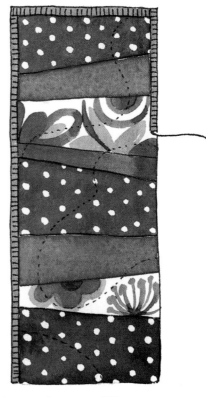

Repeat this at each corner. When you get to your starting point, finish stitching and trim the threads.

Blooming Marvellous Bed Quilt

Don't be put off by the size of this quilt. It is pieced and quilted in four sections, then put together. This makes it less daunting than trying to assemble and quilt a large quilt. The piecing and quilting can be done in a small area, although when the quilt is assembled you do need a large table or floor area.

I delved into my vintage fabric stash for this quilt, but you could use fat quarters. I haven't given the quantity of fabric to buy as it depends on whether you want to use lots of different prints and add your own fabric, or whether you want a more co-ordinated look. For guidance, you will get seven squares out of 6in (15cm) fabric bought from the bolt. For the backing, try to use a small allover print. Each section needs a piece 50in (125cm) square so look for fabric 60in (150cm) wide.

FINISHED SIZE: 81in (205.7cm) square

•Get

❋ 144 x 5½in (14cm) squares of patterned fabric
❋ 44in x 122in (110cm x 310cm) plain fabric for sashing (I used white)
❋ Thread for piecing
❋ 4 x 50in (125cm) squares of fabric for backing
❋ 4 x 50in (125cm) squares of wadding (batting)
❋ 121 buttons
❋ Thread for sewing buttons
❋ Fusible batting tape
❋ Thread to tone with backing
❋ 24in x 44in (60cm x 110cm) fabric for binding
❋ Thread to tone with binding
❋ Rotary cutter, acrylic ruler and self-healing mat
❋ Pins
❋ Sewing machine, ¼in (0.6cm) and walking foot
❋ Iron
❋ Pencil and paper
❋ Masking tape
❋ Quilter's safety pins
❋ Sharps sewing needle
❋ Scissors

••Ready

❋ Divide the 5½in (14cm) patterned fabric squares into four piles of 36 squares, one pile for each section of the quilt. Make sure the colour and pattern of the fabrics are distributed evenly between the piles.
❋ From the plain sashing fabric, cut 40 strips measuring 2in (5cm) across the fabric, selvedge to selvedge. Cut one of these strips into seven pieces, each 5½in (14cm) long. Keep doing this with the strips, until you have 30 pieces 5½in (14cm) long. Place them on to one of the piles of patterned fabrics. Cut 30 more pieces in the same way, and put them on to another pile. Repeat twice more so that each pile has 30 pieces of fabric measuring 2in x 5½in (5cm x 14cm).
❋ Make the strips to go between the rows. Cut five strips 38in (96.5cm) long. Put on one pile. Repeat for the other three piles. Put the remainder of the plain fabric to one side until later.
❋ A ¼in (0.6cm) seam allowance is used throughout this pattern.

••• Sew

1 The quilt is made in four sections, each in the same way. Start by making the top left-hand section. Pick up the squares from one of the fabric piles. Lay them out six across and six down, moving them around until you are happy with the arrangement.

2 Pin then sew the squares together in rows, placing a 5½in (14cm) long, white strip in between. Only insert the white strip between the squares, not at the end.

Press the seams together, facing in towards the patterned fabric.

3 Sew a long strip on to the top of each row, except the top one.

4 Sew the rows together. Use pins to make sure each row lines up, removing each pin as it goes under the presser foot of the sewing machine.

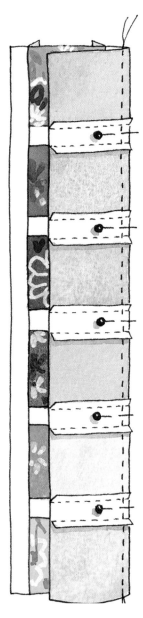

To make it easier to assemble the sections together later on, pin a note on the top right-hand corner of each piece with the name of the section, for example 'Top right'.

Sew the other three sections in the same way. When deciding on the placement of the squares, be aware that the sections will be joined together.

5 Press the four sections. The rows for joining the sections together and the border are now sewn on. Take the white fabric left from cutting the sashing for the sections, and cut the following strips as you sew them on. This stops you getting confused as to what strip is for which side. If your seam allowance has been slightly more or less than ¼in (0.6cm) you may need to alter the length of the strips. It helps to remember the 2½in (6.3cm) strips are only for the border, so are sewn to the outside edges.

Top left

Join a 2in x 38in (5cm x 96.5cm) strip on to the right-hand side; press.

Join a 2in x 39½in (5cm x 100cm) strip on to the bottom; press.

Join a 2½in x 39½in (6.3cm x 100cm) strip on to the left-hand side; press.

Join a 2½in x 41½in (6.3cm x 105cm) strip on to the top; press.

Top right

Join a 2in x 38in (5cm x 96.5cm) strip on to the bottom; press.

Join a 2½in x 39½in (6.3cm x 100cm) strip on to the right-hand side; press.

Join a 2½in x 40in (6.3cm x 101.6cm) strip on to the top; press.

Bottom left

Join a 2in x 38in (5cm x 96.5cm) strip on to the right-hand side; press.

Join a 2½in x 38in (6.3cm x 96.5cm) strip on to the left-hand side; press.

Join a 2½in x 41½in (6.3cm x 105cm) strip on to the bottom; press.

Bottom right

Join a 2½in x 38in (6.3cm x 96.5cm) strip on to the right-hand side; press.

Join 2½in x 40in (6.3cm x 101.6cm) strip on to the bottom; press.

Press each section and trim any stray threads.

6 Make a quilt sandwich from each section, press the backing fabric and lay it out, right side down. Smooth it out so it is flat. Tape the edge of the backing to a table or the floor to help keep it flat. Make sure that it is not pulled too tight. Lay the wadding (batting) on top and smooth it flat. Place the quilt top on the wadding (batting) and backing, ensuring it is positioned in the middle. Use quilter's safety pins to hold the layers together. Starting in the centre, pin every 4–6in (10.2–15.2cm) in rows, to make a grid format.

7 Sew buttons through the layers where the white strips meet, following the photograph on page 111 for guidance. Work methodically from the centre outwards, making sure they are sewn on tightly.

8 It is easier to assemble the quilt if you have space. If you don't have a large floor or table at home, see if you can borrow a friend's table, or use somewhere at work. I have a small local community centre that can be booked by the hour, and sometimes share it with friends who quilt so we can split the cost and we are there to help each other out.

The top two sections are joined together first, then the bottom two are joined together. Finally the two halves are joined.

On each of the four pieces, cut the backing and wadding (batting) 1in (2.5cm) wider than the quilt top all the way around. Pin the edges to keep them in place while you cut. This allows a seam allowance for the sides being joined, and makes the outside border more manageable.

9 Lay the top left piece on a table, right side down. On the side to be joined, gently fold back the wadding (batting) and backing fabric from the front of the quilt. Use quilter's safety pins to hold the layers out of the way.

10 Place the top right section on the top left section, right sides together, and line up the edge of the fabric on the side to be joined. Pin along the strip to stop the fabric from moving, and sew, taking a ¼in (0.6cm) seam allowance.

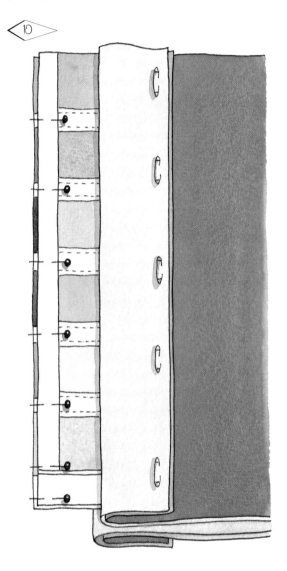

Repeat on the joining side of the top right piece.

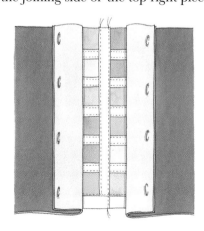

Press the seam allowance to one side.

It can help to place a chair on either side of the ironing board to lay the quilt on to so it is not so heavy on the ironing board and easier to press.

11 Lay the quilt down on a flat surface. Undo the quilter's pins and pull the wadding (batting) free, then fold the backing back and pin to keep out of the way. Fold each piece of wadding (batting) flat so it overlaps. Place an acrylic ruler between the wadding (batting) and the quilt top and use scissors to cut along the wadding (batting), so the edges butt together. (An acrylic ruler prevents you from accidentally cutting through the quilt top.)

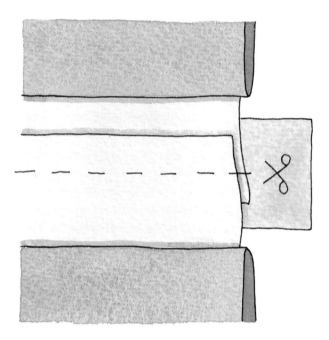

Remove any of the excess wadding (batting) that has been cut away. Pin the wadding (batting) on each side of the join to hold it in place. Lay batting tape over the join. With the iron set to the correct temperature, following the manufacturer's instructions, press to fix the batting tape in pace. If you have a small ironing board, it can help to slide this under the wadding (batting) for when you iron the batting tape.

Note: the ironing board has been kept flat so the wadding (batting) is not stretched by the weight of the quilt. Once the batting tape is fixed, take the pins out that have been helping to hold it in place.

12 Take out the quilter's safety pins holding the backing in place. Lay one backing piece down and lay the other piece on top. On the top piece, fold over ½in (1.3cm) to make a seam and press with your finger. Pin into place. Starting 3½in (8.9cm) from the end, slipstitch to secure, making sure not to sew through to the front. (Leaving 3½in (8.9cm) free helps when it comes to join the top and bottom together.) Stop sewing 1½in (3.8cm) before the end, and secure the thread.

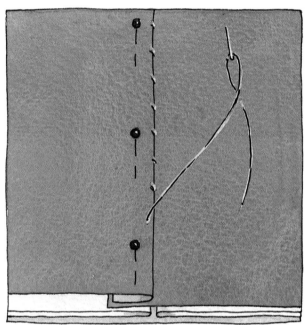

13 Turn the quilt over and sew buttons along the strip just sewn.

14 Repeat steps 12 and 13 to join the bottom left and right sections.

15 Repeat again to join the top and bottom sections together. By this stage the quilt will be large, so rope in a friend to help if possible. After sewing the front seams together, it can help to slide a flat ironing board under the quilt when laid out on the surface (as when ironing the batting tape) as the size can make it a bit of a struggle to take it to the ironing board. When doing the last step of folding over the backing, slipstitch the 3½in (8.9cm) left free when sewing the top and bottom sections.

Take it further

Change the measurements to make a version with larger squares and narrower sashing.

16 Trim the wadding (batting) and backing level with the edge of the quilt top. From the binding fabric cut nine strips measuring 2½in (6.3cm) wide. Join the strips together at a 45-degree angle, to make a length of binding approximately 9¾yd (9m) long. Fold under a ½in (1.3cm) hem at one end of the binding and press. Starting on one side of the quilt, pin the binding to the front with the raw edges together. Start one-third of the way down on one side, leaving a tail of binding 2½in (6.3cm) long, from the end that has had the raw edge turned in. Using a walking foot on your sewing machine, sew the binding to the quilt front, using a ⅜in (0.9cm) seam allowance. Pin the binding in place as you sew each side, removing the pins as they get to the edge of the walking foot. At the end of the side, stop sewing ⅜in (0.9cm) before the edge, and backstitch to secure.

17 Take the quilt from the machine and mitre the corner (see page 28). Pin. Start sewing from the corner, with a ⅜in (0.9cm) seam allowance again. Repeat at the other three corners. When you reach 4in (10.2cm) before your starting point, stop sewing. To finish the binding, tuck the end of the binding in the folded end. Trim the excess binding 1in (2.5cm) beyond the hem so it overlaps. Pin and finish sewing.

18 Turn the quilt over, fold the binding to the back and slipstitch to secure. At the corners, fold the mitre in on the back so it looks the same as the front, and secure with a couple of stitches.

Templates

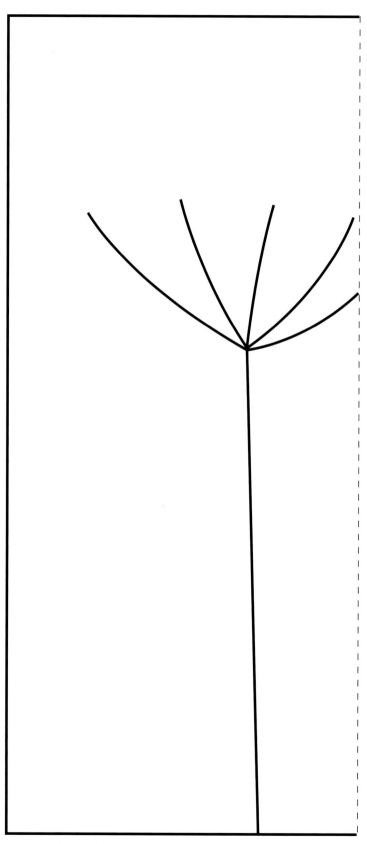

Seed head motifs for Simple Seedheads Table Mat
Enlarge by 141%

Templates

Wedge for Summer Sunburst Cushion
Actual size

Patchwork Rosette Needle Book
Actual size

Tote-ally Fabulous Bag
Actual size

Circle for Summer Sunburst Cushion
Actual size

Funky Town Wall Hanging
Enlarge by 167%

1¼in x 9½in (3.2cm x 24.1cm)

| 1¾in x 3in (4.4cm x 7.6cm) | Window 3in (7.6cm) square | 2in x 3in (5cm x 7.6cm) | Window 3in (7.6cm) square | 1¾in x 3in (4.4cm x 7.6cm) |

2in x 9½in (5cm x 24.1cm)

| 2in x 4½in (5cm x 11.4cm) | Window 3in (7.6cm) square | 2in x 4½in (5cm x 11.4cm) | Door 2½in x 4½in (6.3cm x 11.4cm) | 2in x 4½in (5cm x 11.4cm) |

2in x 3in (5cm x 7.6cm)

Glossary

¼in (0.6cm) foot – A foot for the sewing machine that has a quarter-inch guide on it.

Acrylic ruler – A transparent ruler used for cutting fabric alongside a rotary cutter and self-healing mat. Available in a variety of shapes and sizes, with metric or imperial markings.

Appliqué – A piece of fabric cut to a shape and then applied to another piece.

Backing fabric – The fabric that goes on the back of a quilt.

Backstitch – A stitch sewn in the opposite direction to the previous line of stitching. Used to secure the thread.

Big stitch quilting – A form of quilting that uses thick thread and large stiches.

Binding – The edge of a quilt, which encases the raw edges and looks decorative.

Block – An individual unit that when joined with other blocks makes a quilt.

Border – Fabric sewn around a quilt top to frame it.

Chain piecing – The process of machine sewing pieces of fabric together without stopping to cut the threads in between.

Darning foot – A foot for the sewing machine used for free machine quilting.

Directional print – Fabric that is printed with a design that has an obvious direction, such as a stripe.

English patchwork – A form of piecing where fabric is tacked (basted) to a paper shape before the pieces are sewn together.

Fat quarter (imperial) – $\frac{1}{2}$yd of fabric cut in half across the middle. Measures approximately 18in x 22in.

Fat quarter (metric) – 0.5m of fabric cut in half across the middle. Measures approximately 50cm x 55cm.

Finger press – Using your fingers, instead of an iron, to press fabric.

Fusible web – An adhesive web that, when ironed, glues pieces of fabric together.

Half-square triangle – A square made from two equal-sized triangles.

Long arm quilting – A service where a quilt top is sent to a professional quilter who assembles and/or quilts it on a long arm machine.

Patchwork – Pieces of fabric sewn together.

Perle thread – A non-divisible embroidery thread that can be used for hand quilting.

Quilting – The process of holding the layers of a quilt sandwich together.

Quilt sandwich – A term used to refer to the layers in a quilt – the top, the wadding (batting) and the backing.

Quilt top – The front of a quilt.

Raw edge – The cut edge of the fabric.

Reverse stitch – Reversing the stitch at the end of a row of sewing. Used to secure the seam.

Right side – The printed side of the fabric.

Rotary cutter – A cutting tool that has a circular blade.

Sashing – Strips of fabric sewn in between quilt blocks.

Self-healing mat – A cutting mat that reseals its surface after being cut.

Selvedge – The edge of fabric that is finished to stop fraying.

Tacking (basting) – Long stitches used to hold fabric in place temporarily.

Wadding (batting) – The middle layer of a quilt. Can be made from a number of fibres including cotton, polyester, silk, bamboo and wool.

Walking foot – A foot for the sewing machine that has a set of feed dogs (teeth). Also known as an even feed foot.

Acknowledgments

A huge thank you to all the F+W Media crew who have worked on this book: Carrie for the fabulous illustrations, Heather for her editing expertise, Jeni for her support, and Charly who has made it all look lovely. You have been so supportive and I am honoured to have worked with you all.

Special thanks to Sarah for giving me this opportunity, and being absolutely great to work with, particularly as a first timer.

Two special tutors have been influential on my journey to become a quilter: Sara Cook and Janet Twinn, hope you are proud! Carolyn Clark, your enthusiasm with helping at Quilty Pleasures is immense, you're a star.

Another thanks to Carolyn Clark for long-arm quilting the Grab and Sew quilt using a pantograph pattern designed by Keryn Emmerson.

An appreciative hug goes to the Brighton and Hove Modern Quilt Guild for their tea and chat.

A 'rock and roll' thank you to Lisa and Patrick at Lout for being flexible about my quilting hours.

A big thank you to my family: my mum and dad for their constant support and practical childcare, and to Darren who encourages me all the way and for never complaining about the sewing strewn over the house (well nearly never…). Finally, big love to Jude and Florence for giving me my inspiration.

About the Author

Elizabeth (Liz) Betts runs
Quilty Pleasures, a quilt studio/
shop based in her home town of
Brighton and Hove. As well as
supplying quilters with everything
they need to make a quilt, she
teaches workshops, writes for
magazines and gives talks on the
subject. She has a gentle approach
to quilt making, believing that
enjoying what you are making is
as important as the finished result.
Liz has a background in printed
textile design and has so far
clocked up eleven years of quilt
making. She has had a research
paper published by the British
Quilt Study Group, and is a
founder member of the Brighton
and Hove Modern Quilt Guild.
She has had a quilt featured in
the In The Spotlight gallery at
the Festival of Quilts, which then
toured the UK at the Creative
Stitches exhibitions. Her work is
also exhibited in the Brighton and
Hove Open houses, held every
year in May.

Other passions include music,
particularly going to gigs, and
reading, far too late, into the
night. Liz lives in Hove with her
husband, two children, an old
retired greyhound and a whippet
(each of whom has their own
handmade quilts!).

Suppliers

Some of my favourite places to shop for fabrics and equipment are:

Brighton Sewing Centre
68 North Road, Brighton BN1 1YD
www.brightonsewingcentre.co.uk

The Cotton Patch
1283–1285 Stratford Road, Hall Green, Birmingham B28 9AJ
www.cottonpatch.co.uk

Creative Quilting
32 Bridge Road, Hampton Court Village, East Molesey, Surrey KT8 9HA
www.creativequilting.co.uk

Fabric Rehab
3b Dedham Vale Business Centre, Manningtree Road, Dedham, Essex CO7 6BL
www.fabricrehab.co.uk

Liberty
Regent Street, London W1B 5AH
www.liberty.co.uk

Patch
9 Bevan Street East, Lowestoft, Suffolk NR32 2AA
www.patchfabrics.co.uk

Puddleducks
116 St John's Hill, Sevenoaks, Kent TN13 3PD
www.puddleducksquilts.co.uk

Quilt Me Happy (online only)
www.quiltmehappy.co.uk

Quilt Room
37-39 High Street, Dorking, Surrey RH4 1AR
www.quiltroom.co.uk

Quilty Pleasures
1b Upper Hamiton Road, Brighton BN1 5DF
www.quilty-pleasures.co.uk

Stitch Craft Create
Brunel House, Newton Abbot, Devon TQ12 4PU
www.stitchcraftcreate.co.uk

Tikki
293 Sandycombe Road, Kew Gardens, London TW9 3LU
www.tikkilondon.com

For vintage fabric I visit second-hand shops, go to antique fairs, or buy online from:

Ebay
www.ebay.co.uk

Etsy
www.etsy.com

International suppliers

USA
Hawthorne Threads (online only)
www.hawthonethreads.com

Pink Chalk Fabrics (online only)
www.pinkchalkfabrics.com

Purl Soho
459 Broome Street, New York, NY 10013, USA
www.purlsoho.com

Super Buzzy (online only)
www.superbuzzy.com

AUSTRALIA
Amitie Textiles
103A Gardenvale Road, Gardenvale, Victoria, 3185, Australia
www.amitie.com.au

Ballarat Patchwork
54 Victoria Street, Ballarat, Victoria, 3350, Australia
www.ballaratpatchwork.com.au

My Patch Fabrics
42 Wason Street, Milton, NSW, 2538, Australia
www.mypatchfabrics.com.

Index

American block patchwork piecing 18
appliqué
    Tote-ally Fabulous Bag 40–3
    see also broderie perse

Bag, Tote-ally Fabulous 40–3, 120
"bagging" technique 36–9
batting (wadding) 13, 23
big stitch (utilitarian) quilting 25–6
binding 28–9, 77, 87
    cushions 64–5
    mitred double fold 28–9
    quilts 71, 83, 93
    self 28
    table mats 47
Blooming Marvellous Bed Quilt 110–17
Bookmarks, Spots and Blocks 106–9
Box du Jour 84–7
broderie perse 84–7
bundles 15
button quilting 25

chain piecing 19–20
Charm Packs 11, 48–53
Checkerboard Charms Car Quilt 48–53
colour 11–12
cotton 10, 13
Cushions
    Spinning Around 60–5
    Summer Sunburst 94–9, 120

Dresden plate 94–9

English paper piecing 17, 32–5
equipment 8–9, 21, 24

fabric 10–13
fat quarters 10
Flowered Dolly's Quilt 36–9
Funky Town Wall Hanging 100–5, 121

Grab and Sew Quilt 88–93

half-square triangles 66–71
handles 43
Here and There Quilt 78–83

Jelly Rolls 11, 88–93

labelling 29
linings, bag 43
log cabin designs 72–7
long arm quilters 92

marking tools 9, 24

Needle Book, Patchwork Rosette 32–5, 120
needles 8

Patchwork Rosette Needle Book 32–5, 120
patterns 12
piecing 16–20
    American block patchwork 18
    chain 19–20
    English paper 17, 32–5
    hand 16–18
    machine 19–20
pins 8
pre-cuts 15
pressing 20

quilt sandwiches, how to make 23
quilting 24–7
    big stitch (utilitarian) 25–6
    button 25
    by hand 25–6, 44–7, 105
    straight stitch machine 27, 70
    tie 25, 39
Quilts
    Blooming Marvellous Bed 110–17
    Checkerboard Charms Car 48–53
    Flowered Dolly's 36–9
    Grab and Sew 88–93
    Here and There 78–83
    Twirling Windmill 66–71

rotary cutters/cutting 9, 21–2
rulers, acrylic 9, 21

scissors 8
Scooter Strips Wall Hanging 72–7
seam rippers 8
self-healing mats 9, 21
sewing machines 9
Simple Seedheads Table Mats 44–7, 118–19
Spinning Around Cushion 60–5
Spots and Blocks Bookmarks 106–9
Summer Delight Table Runner 54–9
Summer Sunburst Cushion 94–9, 120

Table Mats, Simple Seedheads 44–7, 118–19
Table Runner, Summer Delight 54–9
tape measures 8
techniques 14–29
templates 118–21
thimbles 8
thread 8
tie quilting 25, 39
tone 12
tools 8–9, 21, 24
Tote-ally Fabulous Bag 40–3, 120
Twirling Windmill Quilt 66–71

wadding (batting) 13, 23
Wall Hangings
    Funky Town 100–5, 121
    Scooter Strips 72–7

A DAVID & CHARLES BOOK
© F&W Media International, Ltd 2013

David & Charles is an imprint of F&W Media International, Ltd
Brunel House, Forde Close, Newton Abbot, TQ12 4PU, UK

F&W Media International, Ltd is a subsidiary of F+W Media, Inc
10151 Carver Road, Suite #200, Blue Ash, OH 45242, USA

Text and Designs © Elizabeth Betts 2013
Layout and Photography © F&W Media International, Ltd 2013

First published in the UK and USA in 2013

Elizabeth Betts has asserted her right to be identified as author of this work in
accordance with the Copyright, Designs and Patents Act, 1988.

A catalogue record for this book is available from the British Library.

ISBN-13: 978-1-4463-0254-5 paperback
ISBN-10: 1-4463-0254-7 paperback

Printed in USA by RR Donnelley for:
F&W Media International, Ltd
Brunel House, Forde Close, Newton Abbot, TQ12 4PU, UK

10 9 8 7 6 5 4 3 2

Acquisitions Editor: Sarah Callard
Editor: Jeni Hennah
Project Editor: Heather Haynes
Art Editor: Charly Bailey
Senior Designer: Jonathon Grimes
Photographers: Jack Kirby and Lorna Yabsley
Illustrator: Carrie Hill
Senior Production Controller: Kelly Smith

F+W Media publishes high quality books on a wide range of subjects.
For more great book ideas visit: **www.stitchcraftcreate.co.uk**